BILKO

BILKO
The Fort Baxter Story

David Thomas and Ian Irvine

Vermilion/Hutchinson

London Melbourne Sydney Auckland Johannesburg

Vermilion/Hutchinson & Co. (Publishers) Ltd

An imprint of Century Hutchinson Ltd

Brookmount House, 62-65 Chandos Place,
Covent Garden, London WC2N 4NW

Hutchinson Publishing Group (Australia) Pty Ltd
16-22 Church Street, Hawthorn, Melbourne, Victoria 3122

Hutchinson Group (NZ) Ltd
32-34 View Road, PO Box 40-086, Glenfield, Auckland 10

Hutchinson Group (SA) (Pty) Ltd
PO Box 337, Bergvlei 2012, South Africa

First published 1985
Reprinted 1985
All 'Bilko' material © Viacom International 1985
Illustrations © Viacom International 1985
Text © David Thomas and Ian Irvine 1985

Set in Century Schoolbook by The Castlefield Press

Printed and bound in Great Britain by
Anchor Brendon Ltd, Tiptree, Essex

British Library Cataloguing in Publication Data
Thomas, David
The Fort Baxter story.
1. Phil Silvers Show (Television programme)
I. Title   II. Irvine, Ian
791.45'72   PN1992.77.P4/

ISBN 0 09 160091 X

Contents

Foreword

On 20 September 1955 the first episode of 'The Phil Silvers Show', otherwise known as 'Bilko', was broadcast by CBS television for New York. In the thirty years since then an entire generation, including the authors, has grown up laughing at life at Fort Baxter. Instantly acclaimed, Bilko has long since joined Inspector Clouseau and Bertie Wooster as one of the great comic originals.

In this book we have tried to capture the essential Bilko. His is a devious, wisecracking, endlessly inventive humour, born from the combination of first-rate scriptwriters working with an inspired star whose fictional character was perfectly tailored to his real-life personality. The inspired collection of supporting characters like Doberman and Colonel Hall provided the ideal foil, and the speed and timing of the show still leave most situation comedies looking flat-footed and sluggish.

In order to track this humour down, we spent months of the most enjoyable research any writers could hope for, watching countless episodes and sifting through scripts. The result is the guaranteed cream of the show's humour. Who could make up anything as good as the original?

'The Phil Silvers Show' is now thirty years old. Only a severe sense of humour failure worldwide will prevent Bilko and Fort Baxter creasing up audiences well into the next century.

David Thomas,
Ian Irvine, 1985

An Interview With Bilko

*I*n the course of our extensive researches into the life and times of Ernest Bilko we naturally journeyed to Roseville, Kansas in search of any archival material that might remain from his time at Fort Baxter. Sad to say, there was not a great deal. We did hear of one profile of the sergeant which had been published by the *Roseville Times* in the late fifties, the paper naturally being interested in such a prominent local figure. We were unable to track down the actual article, but deep in the recesses of the *Roseville Times'* file there came to light the written transcript of the interview that Sergeant Bilko gave to the paper's reporter as he prepared his profile. We reprint it here because we feel it gives a fascinating insight into the way that the sergeant's mind worked at that period. It is in places a stormy interview. The sections on Bilko's war record in particular show that the interviewer seemed well able to stand his ground in the face of his subject's charm and downright dishonesty. We hope that you will be as interested in the following conversation as we were when we first came across it in that dusty office in Roseville.

BILKO   I'm sorry I'm late. I was up all last night mourning for my late uncle Felix. It was a tortuous night.

TIMES   Oh, I'd been told you were playing poker.

BILKO   It wasn't a poker game. More of a wake with deuces wild. Old uncle Felix would have wanted it this way.

TIMES   I'm sorry to be intruding on you so soon after your bereavement.

BILKO   I never said he died yesterday. I just heard about it yesterday. Actually he died in 1940. I was just a kid

	when it happened. My family wanted me to wait until I was old enough to stand the shock.
TIMES	Were you able to sleep in today and rest?
BILKO	Sleep? How can I sleep when there are bugles blowing and men marching up and down. Besides, once I'm up in the afternoon I can never get back to sleep.
TIMES	When would you rise under normal circumstances?
BILKO	I get up at the crack of dawn. Every morning, bright and early, I'm down in the grease pit.
TIMES	Frankly, I don't believe you.
BILKO	O.K., I get up at the crack of noon.
TIMES	Don't you have to deliver your morning report straight after breakfast?
BILKO	I sometimes feel that the whole philosophy of morning reports is open to honest debate between honest men. Why let the enemy know our strength? I must say I go along with Napoleon when he said, 'Keep 'em guessing.'
TIMES	But don't you have a duty to be up and about your business?
BILKO	Well, the way I look at it is, the army pays me to defend my country. I've left strict instructions with Corporal Barbella to wake me up the instant we're invaded.
TIMES	Surely, though, a man of your intelligence would want to be around to get to all the good things first. After all, the early bird catches the worm.
BILKO	You still falling for that old propaganda? Take my word for it. The early bird catches the worm, but it's the smart bird who sleeps late then gets up and talks the early bird out of the worm.
TIMES	Do you ever act like a conventional soldier?
BILKO	Lest we forget, there is a military aspect to the army, too. I take the men out to the drill field, rifle range and on short hikes. Weather permitting, of course.
TIMES	I noticed you were parading some of the men this afternoon.
BILKO	Well, I don't mind a little stroll now and then, but the colonel's on this new parade kick. Every time a big shot is in the area he parades us. What's he so proud of? If I had an outfit like this I'd try to hide them.

2

TIMES So he's been working you hard?

BILKO Walk, walk, walk. To the motor pool – back. To the mess hall – back.

TIMES Does it come as a shock?

BILKO When I was a civilian, I used to see those newsreels of soldiers riding around in jeeps. Every soldier has a jeep in the newsreels. But I joined the army. That was my big mistake. I should have joined the newsreels.

TIMES So what would be your perfect day?

BILKO Up at noon. Then eat. Two o'clock, the finals of the gin rummy round robin. Three o'clock play bingo with map coordinates. Five o'clock all bets in on the new colour of Lieutenant Duber's wife's hair – Corporal Henshaw to report from the camp beauty salon. Then at seven o'clock the canasta tournament, after the finals of the bed-making contest.

TIMES Then lights out at ten o'clock?

BILKO Ten o'clock? I haven't been to bed at ten o'clock since I was six months old and then they had to hit me with a hammer.

TIMES So tell me about your childhood.

BILKO I remember a poker game. It was my first day at kindergarten. I was five years old. We were playing five card stud. My hole card was a deuce of clubs. Little Freddy Dowling had an ace showing, but I instinctively knew that the one to watch was Freckles Hanson who had a king of hearts and a funny look on his face. Now I knew that Freddy's hole card was an ace of spades, because I'd marked it. So when Freckles opened with three jellybeans I raised him a lollipop. Now I knew that Little Johnny Hodges was laying back waiting to sand-bag me with a flush. He was trying to get even because of the crap game I'd been running in the sandbox.

TIMES How about your schooldays?

BILKO I went to high school with Bob Hope's cousin. We were on the wrestling team together. Lovely girl.

TIMES Who would have thought that the young Bilko would grow up and go to war?

BILKO Yes, I've been in some tough situations. There were counter-attacks in the South Pacific where we had to fight for a jeep.

3

TIMES	Then there was Kabuchi Island. You made quite a name for yourself there.
BILKO	Not that again. The court of inquiry definitely proved that the native girl was lying.
TIMES	I was actually referring to the battle at the north end of the island, in which you were involved.
BILKO	Excuse me, but I led my men at the south end of Kabuchi Island. I took the liberty of preparing a small brochure on my part in the battle. You may use my name freely.
TIMES	But the army records state that the battle was at the north end.
BILKO	What's with the north end? Own a little real estate there, bud? I don't care if you want to make a few, but let's stick to the facts. You know, I was mentioned in many despatches.
TIMES	You certainly were. You were the only American soldier who took a Japanese prisoner and tried to hold him for ransom.
BILKO	That's a lie. I was just trying to show the general staff how we could run the war at a profit. Actually I had money on the Japanese to win. This took place years ago. I was young and vibrant then. I had hair.
TIMES	So some things about you have changed, after all?
BILKO	I love jokes about my hair – especially when they're clever like that. I'm not ashamed of the hairs that I've lost in the service of my country. I wear that skin like a badge.
TIMES	How do you feel about life at Fort Baxter?
BILKO	Ah, just think of Fort Baxter, with its shaded walks, the birds at eventide. I love Fort Baxter. I have a pet name for it . . . Siberia.
TIMES	Do you ever face any serious competition from other men at Fort Baxter?
BILKO	No. If they're at Fort Baxter, they're on my property, and when people are on my property they do what I want them to.
TIMES	Tell me about your platoon.
BILKO	There are some outfits that get the sons of millionaires, TV stars, movie personalities. Do they ever send anyone like that here? Oh, no. Do you know how they decide who

comes to this platoon? The army is very careful. They gotta take an intelligence test. Those they find writing with the wrong end of the pencil – that's who comes to this platoon.

TIMES   But you're still very welcoming to them.

BILKO   My room is always open to my men. We have a full line of souvenirs, playing cards and stationery.

TIMES   Is that where you hope they'll spend their money from home?

BILKO   Money from home, money from home. What sweet memories those words evoke.

TIMES   How would you feel if someone else started trying to make money from the motor pool?

BILKO   You know what they call a soldier who tries to make money out of his comrades? They call him a vulture. And there's no room in this barracks for another . . . for a vulture.

TIMES   So you would say that you take care of your men?

BILKO   When the army placed these stripes on my sleeves, they also placed something on my shoulders – responsibility! And what has been my biggest responsibility? The morale of my platoon. I want a smiling barracks. I want my boys to have fun, fun, fun.

TIMES   So you like your men?

BILKO   I do indeed. I like them most on Saturday . . . payday.

TIMES   Of course, the motor pool has quite a bad reputation.

BILKO   You know they've been watching this platoon like hawks since a tank showed up at the beach – sun worshippers!

TIMES   Maybe the motor pool would do better if it volunteered for a few more duties?

BILKO   Volunteer? You know I never allow that word to be used in these barracks.

TIMES   Do you think that your men realize how much you do on their behalf?

BILKO   You love men so much, but they don't appreciate it. They get suspicious. When I think how I rack my brains to think of things to do for them.

TIMES   You mean like betting the entire platoon welfare fund on a losing racehorse?

BILKO	It was like putting it in a bank.
TIMES	But you lost all their money.
BILKO	How was I to know it would lose? It seemed like such a sound investment. The jockey swore that he'd fixed the race. You can't trust anyone any more.
TIMES	What would you say if I told you I had a thousand dollars in my pocket?
BILKO	I can't talk. I'm salivating.
TIMES	You seem obsessed by gambling.
BILKO	You know, when we establish a new military base, the first thing we do is set up a card table. I'm not a pig; we play every day except Monday.
TIMES	Why not Monday?
BILKO	Mondays I go to the bank.
TIMES	Do you have any personal quirks when you're playing cards?
BILKO	I like to pick where I'm going to sit. I need the north light – like every true artist. And I don't like a crowd around. I give the money a chance to breath.
TIMES	What happens when you lose and you have to pay the others?
BILKO	Pay? It's a word I seldom use. I have a rule in life. Never pay what you can talk your way out of.
TIMES	But you must love it when you win, presumably?
BILKO	I don't know why I'm happy when I win. It puts me in a higher tax bracket.
TIMES	I hear you also play Monopoly. Isn't that a bit childish?
BILKO	Not the way I play it.
TIMES	Let's talk about some of the individuals at Fort Baxter. Tell me about Colonel Hall.
BILKO	Nice guy, the colonel. I met him overseas and after the war I sort of kept him with me.
TIMES	He has a great sense of humour. He told me he'd decided to relieve you of the command of this post.
BILKO	Give me a leader with a sense of humour. There are so few. You have to go back to Alexander the Great. You know, I think I'll let the colonel have the jeep this weekend.
TIMES	Then there's Joan Hogan – a fine woman. Will you

marry her?

BILKO   Don't say that. Don't say that even as a joke. I can feel the tension in the barracks every time somebody on the base gets married. I can feel all the eyes on me. I know what they're thinking – that I'll be next. Well, we have an agreement – no GI marriages. She's intelligent, sophisticated. We're too much alike to get married.

TIMES   But do you love her?

BILKO   What are you – the DA?

TIMES   Sergeant Bilko. You're a gambler, a sharpster and a promoter. You're everything a soldier is not supposed to be. And yet people like you. Why is that?

BILKO   I don't know. I guess I *do* have a nice personality.

TIMES   Do you have any worries or problems?

BILKO   Well, you know, sometimes too much charm can be a curse.

Bilko and Colonel Hall

An officer from the Pentagon arrives at Fort Baxter to check that it is suitable for the posting there of Elvin Pelvin and starts questioning Colonel Hall about his ability to deal with crises. The colonel replies: 'I've been in the army thirty years. I've been under fire in two wars, and for the last ten years – thanks to a certain sergeant – my life has been a constant crisis. The Pentagon doesn't have to worry.'

When he leans back in his chair, the colonel's brow unfurrows and he dreams of a smooth-running post, the paperwork under control, and plenty of time for weekends on the golf course and evenings of bridge. Sometimes his ambition occasionally stirs and he dreams of making a coup which will make the Pentagon sit up – like inducting three hundred recruits in record time – and will secure a blessed promotion. But both these desires for a quiet life and professional success are continually frustrated by the presence at Fort Baxter of one man – Master Sergeant Ernest G. Bilko.

By the second episode, 'Empty Store', the relationship between the two is fully worked out: the colonel looks on in amazement at the rewards of wheeler-dealing versus his own blameless and hard-working career. The mess hall provides a huge birthday cake for Bilko ('All I got on my birthday was a jam doughnut'), Signals instal a private telephone for him ('I share mine with fourteen other officers') and Stores tailor Bilko a jacket with pleated shoulders ('Gee, I always wanted one of those').

Bilko for the colonel is an endless exercise in damage limitation: 'We reorganized the entire layout of the post, we moved buildings, blocked off streets, so that no rookie, even by accident, could get near Bilko.' He launches various campaigns to

8

Bilko earning his keep ...

Who really runs Fort Baxter?

Above: Bilko explains to the general, Colonel Hall and Captain Barker how it is that a chimp can be inducted into the US Army ('The Court Martial')

Right: In his command post (otherwise known as the colonel's office) Bilko sweet talks his way around Colonel Hall, and *(above)* Mrs Hall, and *(below)* Joan Hogan

Brothers in arms and cards. Corporal Barbella, Sergeant Bilko and Corporal Henshaw

sweep gambling and other schemes from the post, drafting in personnel from outside Fort Baxter to take on the wily sergeant – tough drill sergeant Quentin B. (for 'Beast') Benson, or pretty Special Services officers to take the men's minds off gambling. But every time he finds himself outmanoeuvred by Bilko's nimble, near-criminal cunning and reduced to despair. And yet . . . and yet . . . we feel that somehow the pair would miss each other. Indeed in 'Transfer' (Programme 22), Bilko moves to another post after being chewed out by the colonel for using his staff car on dates. Bilko is soon bored because his platoon is so gullible that taking their money is no challenge, while his replacement at Fort Baxter is such a rule-book disciplinarian that Colonel Hall yearns for his return and the (reasonably) quiet life.

Again in 'Guinea Pig Bilko' (Programme 133), the sergeant is tricked into taking a tranquillizer which removes his love of money, but the colonel becomes desperate to get things back to normal when Bilko's men, removed from his control, turn into even more rapacious hustlers. He works the cure by getting Bilko to count all the money in the camp treasury – this shock treatment soon snaps Bilko out of it.

When Bilko behaves normally, Colonel Hall can deal with him (more or less) with stoical resignation; when he behaves well, however, the colonel becomes hysterically anxious and prey to the wildest suspicions. When Bilko reforms in 'Bilko Gets Some Sleep' (Programme 49) he is convinced that his motor pool sergeant intends to murder him.

So what is the true nature of the relationship between the two men? The Jeeves and Bertie Wooster of the Mid-West? The Tom and Jerry of the US Army? Perhaps it is really one of the oldest of comic partnerships: that of the bumbling master and wily servant, found in ancient Greek comedy and well mined for laughs by Plautus and Shakespeare among many others. Their affection for each other shows through from time to time. The colonel shows real concern for Bilko when he thinks he has gone down with a dangerous disease in 'Bivouac' (Programme 14), just as Bilko helps the colonel out of various scrapes (which admittedly he has played a large part in causing). He helps him regain the affections of his wife, tries to arrange a promotion by getting him into President Eisenhower's golf foursome, and when off to Hollywood promises he will get Spencer Tracy to play the colonel in the film of *Bilko on Kabuchi*.

The permanent headache Bilko gives Colonel Hall prevents him from slipping into torpor in his sleepy Mid-West post, while for Bilko the colonel is a comfortable and containable representative of authority.

The scriptwriters at the end of the fourth season (and the end of the entire series) finally award the match to Colonel Hall in a show called 'Weekend Colonel' (Programme 142).

Television technology comes to Camp Fremont and Colonel Hall is delighted that the closed-circuit cameras make it impossible for Bilko to run any gambling rackets. He breaks up a crap game in the experimental gas chamber and gloats that Bilko will be on his TV set 24 hours a day. A week later Captain Barker remarks that there hasn't been a card or dice game on the post all week and the colonel turns from watching Bilko hard at work on TV to say that if there was it must have been on radio.

Secure in his triumph, he goes for a weekend with his wife in Lake Tahoe, leaving Barker to watch the TV. Bilko is frantic and complains to Barbella over lunch in a dilapidated roadside diner: 'The colonel's gone, but he left CBS behind. Let's face it, I've become a listening habit.' He orders a burger and does a double-take – the diner's chef is an exact double of Colonel Hall. His agile imagination conceives a plan to turn the tables: 'My own colonel! Something I've always wanted.'

But if the cook, who is called Charlie Clusterman, looks like the colonel, he certainly doesn't act like him. He likes girls and bad jokes, sometimes both together. For example, he asks out the waitress for a little bowling. She refuses. 'That's a shame,' he says, 'with those beautiful pins you're right down my alley.'

At first Clusterman refuses to impersonate Colonel Hall; he'll get ten years if he's caught. But then his bookie appears, asking for $150 that he owes him. 'How much time you gonna give me?' asks Clusterman.

'That depends on how much pain you can take,' replies the bookie.

Clusterman is convinced; he'll be the colonel for $150. He's not ideal for the part – 'Why can't I wear a nice blue uniform?' he asks Bilko.

'Because that's a navy uniform, Charlie. It's little mistakes like that you've got to watch.'

Once at Fremont he makes grabs at all the WACS, but still manages to convince everyone that he's the colonel arrived back early from Lake Tahoe. His first act is to order the removal of the closed-circuit TV, much to Barker's amazement. Then Bilko gets greedy, and has Clusterman announce a Monte Carlo night of gambling, with proceeds going to an undisclosed charity. While Captain Barker lets rip with $200 bets on the dice, the colonel and his wife have returned from their weekend early and stop off at

Charlie's diner for some coffee. They flee rapidly when the waitress calls the colonel a deadbeat and tells him to put on his apron, make a batch of french fries and drain the fat off the chow mein. Back at the base they settle down for bed.

The evening's takings are $1142 at the officers' club and Barker insists on escorting Charlie to the colonel's house with the money. Confronted by Mrs Hall, Charlie hides in the kitchen and when Bilko, Rocco and Henshaw arrive the real colonel answers the door. He denies knowing anything about any money and Bilko is winding himself up to pulverize him, when Mrs Hall comes in.

Realization of his situation inspires Bilko to pretend he has been hypnotized by Henshaw and unaware of what he was doing. This convinces the colonel until Barker arrives and together they piece together the story. Remembering what happened at the diner, the colonel goes there, confronts Charlie and takes the money. Bilko, Barbella and Henshaw arrive at the diner and, with the inevitability of Greek tragedy, incriminate themselves talking to the colonel, thinking that he is Charlie.

The final scene is not a happy one for Bilko fans. Colonel Hall and Captain Barker are revealed gloating over a television screen where we see Bilko and his henchmen glumly behind bars: 'A wonderful show, isn't it, Barker? And the best part of it is, as long as I'm the sponsor it will never be cancelled!'

From the guardhouse a depressed Bilko grimaces and says: 'Th . . . th . . . that's all folks!'

This is a sad state of affairs, a final moral ending with the triumph of a less likeable colonel as avenging authority over a broken Bilko, the spirit of anarchic irresponsibility and fun. How much better to recall the earlier happier days when Bilko's insincere flattery was balanced by the colonel's wry fatalism and near sublime consciousness of the impossibility of converting his motor pool sergeant to a soldier.

Bilko and Gambling

Bilko reminisces, like many an old soldier, about his time in the war under fire and about the instinct he developed: 'I could tell there was something going on, I just knew it. In 1944 in New Guinea I remember right before the Jap counter-attack I had the same feeling and sure enough there it was right in the front line – a crap game! I won $100. It would've been more if it wasn't for that Banzai charge.' This instinct, honed through years of experience in the army, has turned Fort Baxter into, as Colonel Hall describes it, 'Little Las Vegas'. In 'The Twitch' he described his post for the benefit of Captain Whitney, the eager new Special Services officer: 'They'll bet on anything – what I eat for breakfast, for example. I look at an egg and see Bilko collecting from someone who bet on porridge. After lights out the main problem is crap shooting.'

'In the dark?'

'Luminous dice. An invention of Bilko's. I had Corporal Barbella up on a charge for gambling and the motor pool ran a sweepstake on what punishment I'd give him.' Whitney is unwilling to believe that nothing can be done. What about the Morale Officer?

'He came down with melancholia.'

Folk dancing?

'Someone brought in hostesses and started charging 10 cents a dance.'

Woodworking?

'The men worked like beavers for a week – and built a crap table.'

At this point Captain Whitney suggests that what the men need is culture. The colonel looks doubtful, and Whitney goes on to explain that his wife has given a lecture on the life and works of Ludwig van Beethoven seven times at other camps, all of which have been great successes. The colonel is still dubious, but agrees to try it and orders Bilko to ensure that the lecture hall is full for the string quartet concert followed by the talk. Back at the barracks, Bilko uses all his fast-talking talents to offload the tickets: 'When I think of how I rack my brains to think of things for you guys . . . I've got here some free tickets – free, that's a word I don't use so often – for a (mumble, mumble) so come and get them.'

The men are curious and queue up, but hand back the tickets in disgust when they read them. Bilko tries harder: 'Beethoven – hot lips Beety they used to call him . . . Stravinsky – that's Minsky – he went back to his old name.'

No success. But then someone mentions that Mrs Whitney is nicknamed 'The Twitch'; he saw her talk at another camp giving the same talk and during it she nervously tugged her skirt twenty-two times. An argument starts with another soldier who says he also saw it and that she twitched much more.

Bilko at this point with an artist's skill intervenes and opens a book on the number of twitches. The number of bets increases and the stampede for tickets is overwhelming – by Saturday night they are changing hands for large sums. Bets are pouring in – from Tokyo and Germany; four busloads of soldiers arrive at Fort Baxter from Arizona and two who hitch-hiked from Texas.

Information on the Twitch's previous form also arrives – like the time she broke the record in Manila, 'but it was a murderously hot night, half the twitches were mosquitoes'.

By Saturday evening the excitement around the camp is like the world heavyweight boxing title is being contested there. The colonel is overwhelmed with the response – but also suspicious. The talk begins and a commentator outside one of the windows keeps the worldwide audience informed of Mrs Whitney's progress through the services signal network: '. . . and that's the sixth tug and she's not even breathing hard . . . she's started out free and easy . . . and another tug! that's the seventh . . .'

The colonel's unease leads him outside and round to the commentator's window, just as Mrs Whitney finishes her celebrated exposition of Beethoven.

'And it's over, she's finished. Twenty-five tugs! A new indoor record.'

Colonel Hall pulls the plug on the radio.

Later, in despair, he talks to Lieutenant Wigman about the necessity of ridding the camp of gambling, 'not starting another

Belmont, Virginia'. Wigman suggests he might give his talk on Modern Painting – The Passion of Picasso. While saying this he nervously tugs his ear twice, at which the colonel covers his eyes.

Bilko's other great gambling coup came when he and the platoon were attached to Schmill University ROTC to teach motor pool techniques. Bilko loves the place, as he tells the dean: 'My men and I have been on this campus less than ten minutes and already the spirit of Schmill is in our blood.' He tries to organize a Welcome Visiting Soldiers Dance, but the dean tells him Schmill is not coeducational.

'I've taken care of that. I've made a tie up with the local bus to bring certified hand-picked young ladies from town. They'll need somewhere to change because they're picked up right at the pickle factory. It's hard to dance in those rubber boots.'

The dean places Justin Pierce, a student, under Bilko's care. Pierce needs some discipline, the dean thinks, because he gambles. Bilko warms to him when he learns that Pierce's father is chairman of Pierce Steel Corporation.

'The son of a millionaire *and* he gambles? Good boy!'

Bilko takes the dean at his word. He tells Henshaw: 'I've got to show this kid there are other things in life than poker. I gotta show him there's gin rummy, black jack, fantan, schemanderfer, and if time permits, I may introduce the boy to the mysteries of two-card kayoodle.'

Bilko is about to start playing gin rummy with Pierce when a heavy from Ed McMillen's gambling syndicate comes to collect a thousand dollars from the boy. It then dawns on Bilko that Pierce has no money – his father worked his way through college and so must he. Bilko decides to help Pierce from entirely unselfish motives (Pierce becomes president of the steel firm in two years). 'You mean you're going to pay the thousand?' Pierce asks.

'Pay? It's a word I seldom use. I have a rule in life, never pay what you can talk your way out of. Now remember, just because I'm saving your inheritance, don't go hog wild with a vice-presidency. Just anything with an expense account and a fun-loving secretary.'

Down at Ed McMillen's office, however, Bilko is unable to persuade the big wheel to ease up on Pierce. McMillen thinks he can get $10,000 from Pierce's father to keep it out of the paper. After insulting Bilko and his men he has them thrown out.

Back at Schmill, Bilko totals up all the insults: 'tin soldier' – $500, 'cornball uniform' – $1000, 'army slobs' – $2000, 'gold-bricker' – $500 and decides he is going to take McMillen for $4000 *and* make him eat the list of insults.

At this point, the Schmill Football Team make their appearance – composed of small, anaemic types, this is the best side the college has ever produced. In the football season's opening game against Notre Dame University, Schmill have never lost less than a hundred points to nil in fifteen years.

Bilko hatches a scheme and raises $100 from the platoon: 'Ten bucks a piece for the privilege of seeing big shot Ed McMillen a sweating, shaky, broken man, begging us to let him buy back the bet, eating this paper – in which he called you army slobs.'

Down at McMillen's again he places a bet on Schmill to beat Notre Dame with the odds McMillen offers of 1000 to 1. McMillen takes it and tells Bilko to 'beat it, dog face'. Bilko calmly takes out his list and writes 'dog face' down saying: 'That'll cost you another thousand.'

Bilko takes up the post of assistant coach of the Schmill team and transforms their image with some magnificent PR. The senile coach Abernethy he transforms into 'The Old Fox'. The quarterback Cyril G. Hush Jr, weight 126 lbs, becomes 'Swivel Hips Hush' tipping the scales at 200 lbs, Schuyler Van Twitzel becomes 'Crazy Legs Twitzel' 290 lbs, Dexter Lauderdale is renamed 'Ox' and told that he weighs in at 240 lbs. Bilko tells the seven men in the line that 'from now on they will have no names. Immortality will record them as the Seven Rocks of Gibraltar. No individual weights, just an even five tons.'

McMillen is laughing with his hoods when he reads the headline 'Fast Heavy Schmill Eleven Poses Threat For Notre Dame' and suddenly he gets nervous. He calls his contact near Fort Baxter, Blinky Newman, who tells him that 'if Bilko bets, it's a thousand to one he's got inside information'. When the radio confirms the news headline, McMillen decides to go over and buy back the bet.

Down at the stadium he first offers $200 but when Bilko refuses and telephones the sports outfitters saying the uniforms and shoes are too small he goes to $600. Bilko still refuses and telephones an order for cast-iron tackling dummies. McMillen storms out when Bilko tells him he wants $5000 and to watch McMillen eating his words.

The following day the press speculation is intense – 'Experts Climb On Schmill Band-Wagon', 'Smart Money Favours Schmill' – and McMillen is in a panic. He goes back down to Schmill just as Bilko is telling the press that Schmill are so dangerous that only pro footballers will scrimmage against them. The 'pros' then appear saying they won't go on again. Bilko begs the press not to print this or else Notre Dame might not show up.

McMillen is now so frantic he will agree to anything and promises $10,000 cash in half an hour.

While he goes to fetch it Bilko is called to the dean's office. The faculty are impressed with the new spirit on the campus that the football team has inspired and tell Bilko that Schmill *will* win. The fine scientific brains of the faculty have been working on the game. Professor Tuggins, the best mathematician in the country, has been working on some plays: by using the Hadalian laws of moving objects, augmented by Engel's Law of Calibrated Distance, these plays can place all eleven Schmill players in front of any Notre Dame player before he can take a step. The professor of law has discovered eleven loop-holes in the football rules which allow them to put fourteen men on the field. The psychology professor has found a laboratory tested sound which when hummed by the Schmill players will depress, demoralize and bring on a state of complete melancholia among the Notre Dame players.

Overwhelmed by this news, Bilko gets back to the stadium in time to prevent McMillen handing over the $10,000 and to explain to the platoon that Schmill can't lose. McMillen is led away weeping.

Just before the game, a confident Bilko introduces the faculty professors to the team only to discover that their calculations were based on the newspaper publicity. When told his team doesn't stand a chance, Bilko asks if there is anything science can do for them and receives the reply: 'Yes. There have been great advances in first aid.' In a panic Bilko gets hold of McMillen and offers to cancel the bet, but McMillen is a broken man beyond redemption and says that he deserves the punishment.

The game takes place and afterwards the Schmill dressing-room is filled with cheering players – for the first time in their history Schmill have kept Notre Dame down to 99 to nil. They disappear to celebrate, revealing Bilko and McMillen glumly side by side staring into empty space. McMillen says he has decided to buy into a laundry with his brother and give up the gambling racket. He gives Bilko Pierce's IOU and Bilko gives McMillen the list of insults.

There is a moment of silence and then they both start eating the papers.

Bilko and the Arts of Love

Although perhaps best known as a businessman and
entrepreneur, Ernest G. Bilko is also something of a lady's
man. The charm and plausibility that lie at the heart of his
commercial schemes are also the key weapons in his armoury of
love.

As one might imagine, Bilko's powers of flattery are well-nigh
overwhelming. One of his most constant targets, and as a result
one of his staunchest defenders, is Nell Hall, the colonel's wife.
But the other ladies of the camp are also liable at any moment to
be subjected to a torrent of honeyed words.

For example: in the magnificent 'Twitch' episode Bilko has been
summoned (most certainly not invited) to a party at the Halls
where he is to meet Captain and Mrs Whitney, who have plans to
take his and his men's minds off gambling. Bilko determines to
deflect attention away from his misdemeanours by concentrating
on the womenfolk. As he greets Mrs Hall he says, 'Hello, Miss –
the colonel didn't tell me he had his daughter visiting. Why! It's
Mrs Hall! If you get any younger we'll lose you to a rookie.'

As she sits down the barrage continues, 'Mrs Hall, you make a
sofa a throne.' And later, speaking of Mrs Hall to the other ladies:
'What she can do with two eggs is amazing. She's a Paganini of the
stove. I tell you, she has green thumbs.'

Not that the others are left out: 'They are lovely . . . lovely.
When there's so much beauty one gets carried away. You girls
don't give us bachelors a chance. You're lovely – you savages,
you.'

Then, as Mrs Whitney, plain, dark and dumpy, calls out in her
shrill, nasal tones, he begs her: 'Don't tell me . . . I know I heard
you on the Broadway stage. Only one who had been on the stage

17

could speak with such authority and tone. She's perfect for Camille, don't you think, ladies?'

Now this is all very well by way of light-hearted conversational foreplay but sterner stuff is needed for serious romancing. The best illustration of Bilko's seduction techniques comes in 'WAAC' (Programme 10). Bilko has learned that another master sergeant is competing with him for a job that – as he alone has noticed in the small print – carries with it the use of a jeep. The sergeant's name is Hogan. Bilko plans to take his fellow NCO out on the town in an attempt to persuade him to withdraw his job application, little realizing that the sarge is in fact a woman, the lovely Joan Hogan.

He is in for many more surprises, the first of which is that Sergeant Hogan knows all about him, having learned of his reputation during her time at Fort Collins, one of Bilko's previous bases.

'They still tell stories about the things you did there,' she says admiringly.

'Lies! Lies and exaggerations!' Bilko replies, but Joan is not to be deterred.

'They couldn't be. Only one man could have the brains to think of that.'

'Please.'

'I guess because I'm such a silly ninny, a man as smart as you – well – you've been a sort of hero to me.'

The flattery has been turned back on the flatterer, and worse is to come. For Bilko isn't the only one to now that 'when you're in trouble with the army they let you know it in plain language. But when the army's got something good for you they abbreviate it. It's a sort of game. Like the small print in an insurance policy.' No, Sergeant Hogan has also seen the magic letters PTP on the job form and she too knows what they mean – Personal Transportation Provided.

Bilko is astounded, but soon realizes that he has nobody to blame but himself. As Joan points out: 'I didn't mean to cause you any trouble. I was following one of your own rules. They still have it on a plaque in the day room at Collins. Quote: Learn those army abbreviations and read the small print. Sergeant Bilko, I'd just die if I did anything to make you mad.'

It's too late, the Bilko spirit has already been roused. 'Sergeant Hogan. You seem to be a very nice girl. Withdraw your name. Don't force me to resort to intrigue. You'll be annihilated.'

So the battle of the sexes begins, starting with the Bilko Parade of Paper. For, knowing that a soldier is prohibited from taking up extra duties if fully engaged in ordinary ones, Bilko attempts to swamp Joan Hogan's desk in paperwork. He sends in endless inquiries and requisitions, forms by the dozen, but she is unflappable. Finally he plays his ace – the Emergency Tracer, a regulation that states that if an enlisted man is ever charged for a lost article he can demand to have the records for his entire career checked to see whether he was ever issued with the item in the first place. Bilko lost a barracks bag in 1939. Sowici lost a fatigue hat on Guadalcanal. Pendleton was charged for a set of puttees in 1936 and Grover once mislaid a pair of shoes.

It looks as though the game is up. And so it is, but not in the way that Bilko expects. Hogan counters with a demand for an inventory of the motor pool, right down to the last nut and bolt, not to mention Bilko's personal possessions. And the same applies to Sowici's mess hall and Grover's kitchen. It will take months, and keep each of them far too occupied to drive a jeep. Stalemate has been achieved.

But Bilko refuses to be beaten. He suggests they settle by tossing a coin, or cutting cards. Hogan is only too happy to do so – highest card wins. She starts shuffling and immediately brings back memories of Bilko's distant lovelorn past.

'I seem to recognize that shuffle,' he says.

'Of course,' she replies. 'It's called the Bilko Shuffle. My first sergeant at Collins taught it to me. Emily Gribble.'

Bilko's interest is aroused. 'Emily Gribble. You know, I used to go out with her. Is she still in the army?'

'No, she's a dealer in Las Vegas.'

'I've spent a career creating Frankenstein monsters.'

'Sergeant Bilko. I hope that after I . . . after the jeep has been disposed of . . . well, I'd just die if you didn't consider me your friend.'

But it's too late. Bilko is distraught. 'Friend? How can you call yourself a friend when you mentioned the name of Emily Gribble in front of me. You knew you were plunging a knife into my heart when you mentioned that name. A heart that's been empty since Emily left it.'

'Sergeant Bilko. If there's anything I can do . . .'

Well, all seems to be going well at this point. Bilko has won over the lady's sympathy, nicely seasoned with a touch of guilt. He takes the opportunity to fix a date: that night at eight.

The evening opens with Bilko, assisted by his henchmen, preparing for the great occasion. Rocco, however, has qualms: 'I'm ashamed of you. You never had to stoop to this. Making a woman fall for you so she'll give up that jeep.'

Bilko, however, is not convinced. 'What woman? That's a

19

hooded cobra!'

On one matter, however, there can be no debate – she certainly will fall for him. After all, he's giving her the famous Bilko Blitz for which, as the man himself points out, there is no known defence. 'It's the result of fifteen years of intensive research. The perfect formula . . . a man in uniform, moonlight and music.'

His two most loyal lieutenants (be accurate . . . corporals) take up the tale . . .

'Look at the record. Thirty-seven consecutive knock-outs,' says Henshaw.

And Barbella adds, 'And always the same technique . . . I'm Bilko . . . we get through dancing' – he starts dancing with Henshaw – 'he finds the spot where the moonlight catches his good side and then . . . the sigh. She nibbles.'

'Sergeant Bilko, you're sad?' says Henshaw, girlishly.

'Ah, a sergeant's life is a lonely one . . .' replies Barbella as Bilko.

'A *bleak* and lonely one. Get it right,' demands the real Ernest G.

'A bleak and lonely one. Six stripes . . . they're prison bars around my heart. His hand on her cheek. The first tear falls.'

'You poor man. You're too nice a guy to be lonely,' says Henshaw, falling for his charms.

'Bingo! She's hooked.'

Some of the men still object to his callous disregard for her feelings, but Bilko is adamant. 'She asked for it. Boys, this is more than a jeep I'm fighting for tonight. It's more than my reputation. It's the war of men against women.'

'Perfume?' suggests Henshaw, holding out a bottle.

'Why not?' replies the sarge. 'I'll show her no mercy.'

He should, however, have learned by now that Joan Hogan can take care of herself fairly comfortably. This is something that he learns all too clearly when he turns on the Bilko Blitz for the thirty-eighth time and elicits no reaction at all.

'What happened?' he wonders.

'Nothing,' Joan replies. 'Just a slight case of disillusionment. You, Sergeant Bilko, a man I've always looked up to, looking for sympathy . . . You disgust me!'

'What went wrong?'

'Prison bars around your heart . . . What do you think a woman soldier goes through? There's romance in a man in uniform – but a woman in uniform? That wall between her and every soft and tender emotion she needs. You talk of loneliness! Look at these stripes . . . They're claws holding back every feeling a woman dreams of.'

Bilko is quite overwhelmed: 'You poor kid . . . You're too nice a girl to ever be lonely . . .'

It is, sad to say, yet another example of an old truth; man smart, woman smarter. Bilko has lost his heart – and the jeep with it.

Of course, he *has* won the heart of Joan Hogan. But Bilko is then faced with the serious problem of keeping her without becoming married to her. Just as he is so attached to Hogan that if she leaves, as she does once when he has forgotten St Valentine's Day, he is so distraught that he has to follow her to her home town of Sumter, South Carolina to try and recruit her back into the army and his heart, so it is also the case that he will go to almost any lengths to avoid actual marriage to her.

Typical of his efforts is the story of dinner at the Sowicis'. Alarmed by the fact that he has just been best man at a friend's wedding and that Joan's parents are visiting Fort Baxter for the weekend, Bilko decides to show Joan how terrible married life can be by taking her to dinner with Sergeant Stanley Sowici and his wife and son, a plan so bold as to appal even his own men. 'Sarge, it's brutal,' says Henshaw.

The reason for their trepidation is that the Sowicis' marriage is a disaster area. As Sowici himself says: 'Some guys have all the luck. Their wives run off with other men.'

When we see his home life the reasons for his complaints become clear. His wife pours out a string of complaints, which he totally ignores: 'Do I see anyone, do you ever take me anywhere?'

'Shaddup.'

'Every night we just watch TV. What do I get dressed for – the eleven o'clock news?'

'Shaddup.'

'Shaddup, shaddup, that's all you know. Can't you make conversations?'

'Why didn't you marry Noël Coward if you wanted conversation?'

'Why didn't I marry anybody? I was going to be your little princess.'

Their awful little boy enters, telling his mother to 'shaddup' en route. He wants to take his father outside to prove to his friends that he has the biggest feet on the base. Sowici hits the little brat. His wife is furious: 'Always on the head – what are you, afraid he'll get a few brains and show you up?'

Sowici has just raised his hand to hit the boy again when Bilko enters. 'What a beautiful domestic picture,' he lies, looking around at the total squalor with considerable satisfaction – this is just what he wanted.

'Welcome to Shangri-la,' says Sowici.

'Watch out, he's after something,' warns the little brat, catapulting the first of many pellets onto Bilko's nose.

Bilko explains to Sowici that he wants to take Joan out to the platoon party that night, but he can't afford to take her into Roseville for a proper dinner. So can he bring her over to the Sowicis for dinner? 'Don't go to any fuss,' he says.' Just leave everything as it is and stay as charming as you are.'

The Sowicis are stunned. 'He wants to bring his girl here?' asks Agnes, incredulously.

'He's the first person that ever wanted to come to dinner here,' admits Stanley. 'Including me.'

But Mrs Sowici is inspired: 'It's the first time since we've been married that someone has considered this a home. Stanley, what's happened to us? Look at you, look at me. We fight all the time. Listen, Bilko wants to show his girl a happy family. Let's give him one, even if we have to pretend.'

'When we were first married we didn't have to pretend,' says her husband.

'He's going to see a happy home all right and we won't have to pretend now.'

'What's going on?' wails the boy, who is practically in tears of terror at the sight of this unexpected love between his parents.

'We've got company for dinner,' explains his mother. 'Do you know what that means? No, it was before your time.'

Six o'clock comes and Joan and Ernie arrive for dinner to find that the house has been spring cleaned and hung with the best drapes while Agnes Sowici is wafting about the place in her best party dress. Joan is charmed. Bilko pretends not to recognize where he is. Enter Stanley Sowici in his dinner jacket. Bilko doesn't recognize him, either. 'It's the first time I've worn this since we were married,' says Sowici, rubbing noses with his now adoring wife. He continues, 'I thought I'd get it out. You never know when there isn't going to be another wedding around here,' and he nudges Bilko full in the ribs.

By now Joan is utterly enchanted, 'This is such a happy home.' 'But there seems to be something missing,' remarks Bilko. 'Wasn't there a little animal . . . sorry, a little boy here?'

'Oh, you mean Junior,' says Agnes, and calls for her son: 'Mother's Blessing, Mother's Blessing.'

The boy, wearing cut pyjamas and sucking his thumb, appears in his father's arms. 'Who are the nice people, Daddy?'

Bilko is appalled. 'This kid's been drugged. He's under sedation.'

22

But there is worse to come. As the two couples sit down to dinner Mrs Sowici says that they hired one of the waitresses from the Paradise Bar and Grill to act as a maid. Joan clearly disapproves of the bar, known as the Snakepit to its regular clientel. 'I've never been there,' asserts Bilko. 'I instruct my men not to go near the place. I've told them this many times.'

Enter the waitress: 'Hi Ernie. What happened at the Pit last night? After the chandelier fell down everything went black.'

Bilko tries to deny all knowledge of the woman, but Mrs Sowici is not deceived. 'Bilko, you're a fool. Wasting your time in these awful places when your real happiness is right there beside you. I'm sorry, it's just I know how much my happiness lies with my home and my family, and when I look at you . . . oh!' And she runs crying from the room, closely followed by her husband.

By now Joan, who has been delighted and then furious, is now in tears: 'Don't you ever speak to me again,' she wails and rushes from the house.

Sowici re-enters the room, 'My wife, she's all heart.' Then he notices Joan's absence. Bilko tells him that she left, crying. 'Crying?' says Sowici. 'Ernie, she loves you. Go catch her, don't let your happiness get away. Fly after her!'

Bilko leaves, very, very slowly, calling 'Joan, Joan . . .'

Just then Agnes arrives and wonders what has happened to her guests. 'Let them go,' says Stanley.

'Let them go?'

'Yeah. I don't like a crowd around when I'm with a beautiful girl.'

Agnes collapses, simpering, into her husband's arms, the door closes, the lights go out and at least one marriage on base has been secured.

But the one marriage that really matters to Sergeant Bilko – his own – has still to be saved from taking place. It cannot be done by persuasion. If Ernie states that military marriages end in divorce then Joan has figures to prove that they are more secure than those in the civilian world. If he says that it is a bad financial move, she's right there with the allowances and health benefits that make a union between two master sergeants an entirely profitable one.

There are, no matter what Bilko may do, times when the altar seems perilously close. None more so than in a story that opens one Saturday night with the men of the motor pool clustered around the poker table. Bilko is having trouble keeping his fellow cardsharps away from the charms of their womenfolk. Fender wants to go meet his date. 'But she's not even your girl. She's your wife,' comes his sarge's contemptuous retort. In any case, as Bilko points out, 'The only husband who didn't leave his wife on Saturday to play poker was Adam. And that was only because he couldn't find a game.'

At this point Corporal Henshaw reveals that he has seen Joan Hogan in town with Private Mulligan. Bilko professes to be unconcerned and keeps on dealing the cards. He does not notice that he has dealt all the cards into one pile.

Gradually he admits that he is more than somewhat upset: 'What can I do to make her jealous? I know, I'll go into town and get drunk. But I don't drink. I know – I'll overeat.'

He spends the next hour down at the gates to Fort Baxter pestering the Military Policemen and begging them for any evidence of the missing couple's arrival. 'When they come through we'll fire our rifles to let you know,' says one, but Bilko stays hanging around there all the same.

Eventually Joan and Mulligan arrive, arm in arm and laughing. Bilko continues to feign lack of concern – 'If this is a little manoeuvre to make me jealous you've not succeeded' – but when Joan says that the two of them have been to the movies his true feelings become apparent. 'Where are your stubs? What was the name of the movie? Who was starring? It sounds like a pretty weak alibi to me.'

At this Joan is not unreasonably upset: 'I'm not married to you,' she cries. 'You're a contemptible, suspicious beast. Every Saturday night when you play poker you expect me to sit alone in the barracks. I never want to see you again!'

On the Monday morning the motor pool is not a pleasant place to be. Bilko is kicking and shouting at his men. Mullen objects: 'Just because you had a beef with your girl don't take it out on us.' Meanwhile Bilko is not the only one with girl trouble. Kadowski has also had a lover's tiff and wants to go down to the jeweller's in Roseville to pick up a gift for his girlfriend. This inspires Bilko. He tells Doberman to go down to the jeweller's and pick up a charm in the shape of a doghouse: 'Me, Sarge?' asks Doberman. 'My birthday's not till January.'

Bilko relaxes once Doberman has been sent on his way, all the more so when he comes back and informs the sarge that he has left the package on Joan Hogan's desk. But Bilko's happiness is shortlived, for Kadowski appears, complaining that his package contained the doghouse charm when it should have had an engagement ring. The engagement ring, that is, that has just been left on Joan Hogan's desk. Bilko is desperate. 'Is there a problem?' asks the blindly uncomprehending Doberman.

Bilko in his element, surrounded by beauties ('Bilko F.O.B. Detroit')

Bilko the marriage counsellor – introducing the jealousy factor to rekindle wives' lost passion by *(left)* finding a new maid for Colonel and Mrs Hall ('The Big Scandal') and *(below)* bringing a blonde into the Ritzik household ('Bilko Saves Ritzik's Marriage)

The army makes a soldier out of Zippo the chimp ('The Court Martial') ...

... and Bilko makes a monkey of himself in the Monte Carlo casino ('Bilko Goes to Monte Carlo')

True love prevails ... or does it? Ernie and Joan almost tie the knot ('Bilko's Engagement')

'If she's already opened it, there's no problem. I'll kill you,' replies his sergeant.

In the WAC office the girls are all taking turns to look at Joan's ring. 'After five years I just can't believe it,' exclaims Joan.

Bilko enters. 'There's something I have to explain,' he says.

'There's no need,' says Joan. 'You've just made me the happiest girl in the world.' And she wraps her arms around him in a joyous hug.

Colonel Hall, too, is delighted by Bilko's newfound sense of commitment. 'Ernie my boy, my heartiest congratulations. I've always said that all you need is the steadying hand of a good wife.'

Everyone joins in with the 'happy' couple. Mrs Hall starts planning their reception, which she insists on holding at the colonel's house. The chaplain makes suggestions about the service and Colonel Hall starts ordering their sex life: 'No loafing, you two. The army needs new recruits.'

Joan announces that her folks are on their way up to Roseville for the wedding. 'What are they?' asks Bilko. 'Guided missiles?'

Back with his troops, Ernie Bilko considers the awfulness of the situation. 'Five years of scheming and planning just so the subject of marriage never comes up – now this. The moment she opened the package the bottom of my life fell out. Now the chaplain's starting to clear his throat.'

One of the men suggests he simply cancel the wedding.

'I can't reject her – she's a human being.'

So why not marry her?

'*I'm* a human being.'

At which point Doberman enters and takes his life in his hands; he congratulates Bilko on his engagement.

Bilko realizes that his only hope is to make Joan turn him down. The arrival in Roseville of her parents, who have summoned him to meet them and secure their approval, provides just the opportunity he needs. 'The Bilko we know is irresistible. The Bilko they'll meet is another matter.'

In their hotel room Joan Hogan's parents are hoping that their future son-in-law will be a nice, quiet man. Enter Bilko, wearing a joke mask. He holds out his hand. When the father shakes it he discovers there's a buzzer in it. Then Bilko offers the couple some joke candy. He turns to Mr Hogan: 'Is this your wife? She's a little on the fat side. Did you marry her for her money?' He then devotes his attention to Mrs Hogan: 'That's a great hat. Did you buy it or grow it?'

Mr Hogan then calls Bilko over to him and points at the flower in his lapel. 'Take a good look at this flower,' he says. Bilko bends over it – and is promptly doused in water. Mrs Hogan offers him a chocolate. He opens the packet and a jack-in-the-box pops out. A pair of motorized false teeth start chattering across the table. The parents, it seems, love practical jokes and they adore Ernie Bilko.

Failure there, but perhaps Bilko will have better luck with Joan's two aunts, who have also arrived in town. These two sweet biddies are having a spot of tea when Bilko arrives, clutching a bottle of whisky, swaying from side to side and slurring his speech. They look up, alarmed. 'You think I'm drunk,' he says. 'I'm not – I'm fighting a cold. I've been fighting it fourteen years now. All right, I'm drunk, loaded – so what? Hey, I known you. You're sisters . . . which one's Zsa-Zsa?'

The aunts get up to greet him: 'Don't move. I'll see nineteen aunts.'

The response of the old dears is not, however, quite what he might have expected. 'Don't drink that stuff. Join us – we've been on Martinis all afternoon. Don't worry. We won't tell Joan's folks – they're a nice couple, but square.'

Things are getting serious for Bilko and they certainly don't improve with the news that Mrs Hall is throwing an engagement party for him and Joan on Thursday night. But Thursday is Burlesque night at Minsky's and Bilko is the Iron Man of the Runway. In eight years he has never missed a show: 'He even went when he had broken his glasses and could only listen.' The men are despondent at the news that he will not be there with him: 'But sarge, without you to get us in we'll have to sit way back – in the second row.'

But all is not yet lost. Bilko decides to import an aunt of his own, Tessie la Torso, one of the showgirls. He does some quick calculations; the show begins at seven-thirty, Tessie comes on in the first act; that should leave her plenty of time to get to Fort Baxter and the party by twenty past eight. One sight of such a blatant floozie for a relative should be enough to put the Hogans off him for good.

She certainly seems perfect for the part. As Thursday evening opens she is cat-fighting with another girl at Minsky's who, she says, has stolen her act. 'I wrote to Washington, but they won't let me patent my act. What goes on when your government won't protect you? What is this – Russia?'

Bilko tells Tessie she's going to meet a man who can help her become a serious actress: 'You always wanted to do your own show, now here's your opportunity – *Death of a Salesman* . . . as a musical' – but he explains that she must appear to be respectable.

Bilko leaves and then Paparelli arrives to give Tessie her lift to the camp. By mistake he gives the game away – 'He thinks of you as part of the family' – and Tessie is enchanted: 'Family – no one's ever thought of me as family.'

At Mrs Hall's party everything is going well, but Bilko is nervous. There is no sign of Tessie. Joan's aunts arrive and refuse Mrs Hall's offer of tea – they've brought their own. Finally Tessie arrives, looking prettily demure in a neat dress and with spectacles on the end of her nose. Everyone is delighted by her – except for Bilko – and the colonel is sure that he's seen her somewhere before: 'Is she part of your garden club?' he asks his wife.

Last of the expected guests to arrive is Joan, looking gorgeous. So stunning is she that Bilko thinks to himself that perhaps he might get married after all. Just when he is about to say so Joan gives the plot one final twist. She has decided not to marry him – this party is actually to celebrate Kadowski and his bride. Everyone goes off to congratulate the happy couple, leaving Bilko alone in the room, without even the aunts' teapot of Martinis to comfort him.

Joan returns and Bilko begs her to reconsider her decision, but she is unrepentant: 'When I get married I don't want it to be by mistake – after all, I hardly know you.'

She forces him to promise that they'll always spend Saturday nights together, so it comes as something of a surprise when the final scene opens where the show began, around the poker table with Bilko sounding off to his cronies: 'If you can't persuade your girl that Saturday night is poker night, you're no man.'

It is, however, left to Joan to have the final word as the camera pans back to show that she, too, is seated at the table: 'Shut up,' she says, 'and deal.'

Duane Doberman – Portrait of a Legend

W hat can one say about Duane Doberman, the super-slob
from Altoona? He is the kind of man who visits a cattle
ranch and ends up getting branded, who is so gullible that
if he loses $500 in cash and has it won back by Bilko, he is conned
out of it all over again. Perhaps the best description of him is made
by Bilko himself; conjuring up a vision of the man for the haughty
socialite Joy Landers . . .

'First, you must forget all your conventional middle-class ideals
of beauty. You must forget the tall blond type, which is rapidly
losing favour with the continental set. To describe Doberman we
must take a leaf from the Orient. We must think deeply in the
manner of those who have mastered the arts of love and beauty.
Picture in your mind's eye . . . dark, short, with that pulse-
quickening plumpness – a Buddha. His face glistens as if rubbed
with a mysterious oil. Swarthy, greasy if you will, but with that
inscrutable air about him.'

Well, a little overblown, perhaps, but one of the things about
Doberman is that Bilko is always making him out to be more than
he actually is. When he opens a radio station, Doberman is 'the
dean of American news analysts'. When he wants to impress the
snooty parents of Doberman's girlfriend, Lillian Middleton, he is
'Crown Prince Doberman' over in Roseville incognito to study
American military methods. Bilko puts Doberman in movies, on
television as Tex Doberman, into quiz shows. He even runs
Doberman for Mayor of Roseville, backed up by slogans like 'I'm
Insane About Duane' and 'If You Like Ike, You'll Love
Doberman'.

Doberman's responses to these machinations veer from
reluctance – 'Aw, Sarge' – through petulance, to outright

28

stupefaction, even unconsciousness. All three are illustrated when Doberman is chosen to star as Private All-Thumbs in the training film on 'The Care and Maintenance of the Spark-Plug'. His first reaction is, 'I can't face the cameras, I'll die.' But Bilko, who has persuaded the man from the army films department that Doberman can do the job – 'He has a certain Jackie Coogan quality, when he smiles you could melt' – is determined to teach him to act. He makes Doberman say his one line, 'I just give it a twist with this wrench' and then Bilko bursts into tears – 'With one line he tears your heart out.'

'Was I good?' asks Doberman. Bilko tells him he was a star and Doberman is transformed. 'Sarge, even if I'm a star I don't want you to treat me any different from the rest.'

Bilko affects wonderment: 'Isn't that a grabber? Doesn't that get you right here? The bigger they are, the nicer they are.'

But then comes the crunch; 'Sarge, there's one more thing. I notice I only have one line. Paparelli, who's a nothing, has three lines.' Then, in rehearsal, Doberman refuses to say his line loudly, for fear of ruining his voice, and takes great umbrage when Paparelli suggests he should hold his wrench up higher: 'He's trying to teach me how to act. If you want somebody else to do it that's quite all right by me.'

The truth will out, however, and the truth about Doberman's real talent is all too clear when the real action starts. One look at a camera and he faints dead away.

Nevertheless, there is something appealing about Doberman. It is to him alone that Elvin Pelvin will sing; Doberman's eyes remind Elvin of his hound-dog back home. And Doberman is the only member of the platoon to befriend Montana Morgan, the impossibly boisterous cowboy who joins the motor pool.

We can look for guidance in the stars. Judging by clues given in 'Bilko's Engagement' Doberman is a Capricorn and it is fair to say that there is a certain goat-like doggedness (?) to him, even if he is less of an achiever than one expects from members of that sign.

As to his family, several false clues are laid throughout the series. Doberman is thought to be the missing heir to Lord and Lady Roberts. A general looks very like him, suggesting, perhaps, some youthful and hitherto unadmitted indiscretion. But the truth when it emerges is more mundane. He comes from a small town and has a mother and a sister Diane. This sibling gets Bilko into trouble when, having organized a Family Day at which the men of the motor pool will escort one another's sisters, he finds that no one wants Doberman's. He then tells them that she is a raving beauty, falls for his own spiel, dates her and finds that she is Doberman's identical twin.

Not that his looks prevent Doberman from feeling the most ardent passions. His fevered pursuit of Mrs Hall, with whom he falls in love after Bilko accidentally hypnotizes him, shows to what lengths of telephoning, flower-sending and wall-climbing he will go once properly fired up. And then there is the undoubted depth of his feeling for Bilko himself. Faced with the prospect of Bilko's departure in 'Lieutenant Bilko' (Programme 84) and a request to iron the sergeant's shirts, Duane replies: 'I can't do it. Every stroke of the iron takes you farther and farther from me. Before I met you I was nothing but a slob.' Bilko responds with affection mixed with exasperation. For example, when Doberman, having got Pelvin to sing, then sings along with him, thus ruining the motor pool's recording of the star, Bilko is asked whether he wants the recording equipment turned off. He replies, 'No, leave it on. We've got an album here – "Duane Doberman Sings Us Out of a Fortune".'

A story which encapsulates almost all of the key elements in Doberman's character and Bilko's handling of it is 'Mardi Gras' (Programme 21). The show opens with the motor pool decorating their float for the annual Mardi Gras parade and picking the king of the Mardi Gras who will reign over them, together with a queen of his own choosing. Bilko puts all their dog-tags into a helmet and draws out . . . Doberman's. As always, Duane's nerve immediately fails him.

'Sarge,' he pleads, 'I can't be no king.'

'Whaddya mean you can't be, you'll be great,' Bilko assures him. 'Look at you. You're royal, you're regal. You're a small Farouk. And now, Your Majesty, we breathlessly await your first command. Who, sir, shall be the lucky lady who will reign as your queen?'

Silence.

'C'mon, c'mon Doberman, who's the lucky girl?'

'Girl?' replies the wretched ruler. 'Aw, sarge . . .'

'His Highness is a bundle of nerves. We, your loyal subjects will pick your queen for you. Now, Your Majesty, go and get washed up. Then go over to the welding shop and get fitted up for a crown. On the double – hey-oy-yup!'

The problem of finding a consort for King Doberman is soon solved when his locker is revealed to be full of cuttings and pictures of Joy Landers, Roseville's most beautiful debutante, who has just been on a trip to Paris. 'I know that this is just Doberman's dream,' says Bilko. 'But this year Doberman is king. This year dreams come true.'

Rocco Barbella, as head of the Coronation Committee, is sent off to Miss Landers' house to read her the proclamation that King Doberman the First has chosen her to be his queen. Doberman returns to be told that a queen has been found to share his throne. 'What – a girl?' he asks.

'No, a chipmunk.'

Bilko tells Duane that there's a girl in Roseville who's been worshipping him from afar – even driving up to Fort Baxter in the hope of sneaking a glimpse of him. They have decided to give her a break and make her the queen. Who is she? Why, Joy Landers.

Doberman faints.

Meanwhile the smart set of Roseville's *jeunesse dorée* are talking to Joy Landers about her time in Paris. She turns out to be arrogant and spoilt. ('We are a small island in an ocean of yokels,' she tells her friends.) When Corporal Barbella and the other members of the Coronation Committe arrive to read their proclamation she laughs at them and sends them away with the remark that there must be some shopgirl in town who'd be very happy to be their queen.

Back at Fort Baxter all is not well with Doberman. 'I don't understand it,' says Bilko. 'You've got eight campaign ribbons, two battle stars, but when it comes to meeting a girl you fall apart.' He desperately tries to get him to practise making a suitably royal greeting to Miss Landers: 'Go on, like a king, with your head erect and proud.'

Private Mullen enters in drag: 'Well, if it isn't Mr Duane Doberman.' But Doberman can't go through with it and pleads to Bilko: 'Sarge, I don't know what to do around girls, I'm scared.'

Bilko tries to explain that it's very easy to cope with girls. You simply talk to them. When Doberman replies that he doesn't know what to talk about Bilko suggests Paris. 'You've been to Paris. Tell her what you saw in Paris.'

'What did I see? I was in a Sherman tank.'

Bilko keeps trying. He sends King Doberman out to meet the imaginary Miss Landers. 'Well, if it isn't Duane Doberman,' 'she' repeats.

At last Doberman manages a word: 'Hello'. The platoon cheer.

'Did you hear that?' Bilko asks his men. 'Did you hear the way he said hello? Oh, the poor girl's going to melt.'

No she isn't. Because at this point the Coronation Committee returns with the bad news that not only did Joy Landers turn them down, but she also laughed in their faces. 'Nobody laughs at my platoon,' announces Bilko. He decides that Doberman is going to be given the chance to turn her down in return. 'When I get through with her she's going to want Doberman more than any woman has ever wanted any man. It will be the crowning achievement of my career. I'm going to have a short talk with Joy Landers. I want to meet Miss Laughing Girl.'

He bursts into the Landers' drawing room and pretends to apologize for the presumption of his men in asking her to be the queen of 'some ridiculous little affair that they're running'. 'Turn them down!' he insists. 'Those poor fools made Doberman king of the Mardi Gras without his knowledge. You can't blame them with their drab army lives. When this international figure appeared, well naturally they wanted to show him off, not realizing that he went into the army for the sole purpose of getting away from the terrible pursuit of him by women.'

Ignoring any interruption Bilko continues: 'Please leave him alone. Respect his desire to be just an anonymous soldier and not Duane Doberman of Paris, the Riviera, that unfortunate suicide attempt by that beautiful countess, that chase across four continents. Please – leave him alone! Just for that momentary flash of international fame that this would give you, please don't turn our wonderful, sleepy little town into a bedlam of newsreel cameras, reporters, souvenir hunters. As an old army sergeant I beg you: don't turn our army camp into a rendezvous for women of all nations. It's not too late. I beg you, turn it down. Refuse to be queen of the Mardi Gras.'

'I already did,' replies the bemused socialite.

'Beg your pardon. Miss Landers, are you trying to tell me that you actually turned down the opportunity of having your name coupled with Duane Doberman?' He sniffs and reaches for a handkerchief. 'Forgive this outburst of emotion, but I thought that old-fashioned decency and courage were disappearing from the American woman. You're a big woman to realize that those endless nightclubs, the parties with Princess Margaret, the flights around the world in Doberman's private plane. They're not for you. This is where you belong.'

By now Joy Landers, who has desperately been asking 'Duane who?' throughout Bilko's diatribe, is in a state of total consternation. He leaves as her boyfriend enters ('Is this your boyfriend? Solid, a bit slow . . . you have chosen the right path, my dear') and passes her father on the way out. The old man apologizes for his daughter's despicable behaviour towards Bilko's men and says that she needs a good lesson; she's been spoiled. Everything she has ever wanted she has got.

'Well,' says Bilko, 'There's something she wants now more than anything else in her life and she ain't going to get it.'

Colonel John T. 'Melonhead' Hall

The world's greatest lover: Duane Doberman demonstrates his inimitable way with women

Above: with two glamorous Wacs in 'Operation Love'; *(right, top)* with a millionaire's daughter in 'His Highness Doberman' and *(right, bottom)* with a bar-room siren in 'The Con Men'

The lovely Joan Hogan

'What's that?'

'Doberman.'

Phase two of the operation begins. At the Chinese restaurant where she is dining Miss Landers receives a fortune cookie: 'It is better to have loved Doberman and lost than never to have loved Doberman at all.' The Roseville smarties move on to the Club Carribbean, where they are entertained by a calypso that goes as follows:

'In Jamaica where we come from,
We hear of lovers one by one,
Rubirosa and Ali Khan,
But the greatest one is Doberman.

Chorus
Doberman, Doberman, de greatest one is Doberman.

One night down in Venezuela,
He was chased by Lollobrigida,
Princess Margaret don't want de throne,
All she wants is Doberman.

Chorus
Doberman, Doberman, all she want is Doberman.

There'll be newsreel pictures and worldwide fame,
To de girl who captures de fascinatin' Duane,
Women weep and carry on,
Oh where oh where has Doberman gone?

Chorus and finale
Doberman, Doberman, oh where oh where has Doberman gone?'

This is too much for Joy and when she hears two soldiers saying that Doberman is going down to the Paradise Bar and Grill that night she is determined to follow him there despite the protests of her snooty friends that the place is just a cheap joint for soldiers.

Over at the Paradise, Bilko is trying to persuade a reluctant Doberman to go through with his plan for the good of the platoon.

'I'll die, I'll die,' pleads Doberman, overwhelmed by the thought of coming face to face with Joy Landers.

'No you won't. You'll be magnificent,' says Bilko, as Doberman is hustled off to hide in the washroom.

Joy Landers arrives, only to meet Mildred, the bar's owner, who is disguised as a countess, who has travelled to Kansas in search of Doberman and who is furious at the thought that Joy may beat her to him. By now Joy is almost overcome by excitement. She begs Bilko to describe the great lover to her, which Bilko – as we have seen – does to startling effect. She cannot wait for Doberman to arrive and announces to the world that she has changed her mind and wants to be queen of the motor pool Mardi Gras. Henshaw is sent to fetch Doberman while Joy trembles in anticipation.

Finally Doberman arrives, almost paralysed by nerves and having to be supported by two other soldiers for fear that he may collapse. A cigarette-holder is sticking out of the corner of his mouth. He looks ghastly. But Joy Landers sees nothing but the playboy image that Bilko has created. 'He is magnificent,' she says.

Bilko introduces Miss Landers to Private Doberman. 'This is the happiest moment of my life,' says the girl, but the great man remains silent.

'Private Doberman, won't you say something to the young lady?' asks the sarge.

'Get lost,' comes the reply.

'Who is this man?' demands one of Miss Lander's friends.

Bilko tells him: 'This man is Private Doberman. Just plain Private Doberman – no yachts, no women chasing after him, just a nobody like the rest of us. A nobody who doesn't enjoy people laughing at him. A nobody who now says – say it Doberman . . .'

'Get lost.'

After this rare moment of naked cruelty, matters might have ended on a rather sour note, but for the fact that in a postscript Miss Landers turns up at the motor pool, where the men are laughing at her public humiliation. She apologizes for her haughtiness and then sets about lending a helping hand: 'I may not know much about humility, but I do know how to run a party and this is going to be the greatest Mardi Gras Roseville has ever seen!'

Bilko announces that the Mardi Gras still needs a queen. He turns to Doberman and asks, 'Your Highness, do you accept this lady as your queen?'

'Hello,' comes the meek reply.

Aaah, a happy ending. How nice.

Bilko, Hollywood, Broadway and Television

*T*hroughout his distinguished military career Bilko has often shown signs of perhaps leaving the army and pursuing a career in some other field. Banking on Wall Street has engaged his interest (Programme 34), as has running a nightclub (Programme 78), owning a chain of Chinese restaurants (Programme 99), selling potato sacks (Programme 113), managing a hotel (Programme 124) and building automobiles (Programme 136). Nothing, however, has come so often between the sergeant and his service to his country as show business in its many forms.

As early as Programme 13, when Bilko went to Hollywood as adviser to Cecil D. Chadwick on his film of *Love In a Foxhole*, he has shown that, given the chance, he would use his immense talents in the motion picture industry. In 'Bilko's Hollywood Romance' (Programme 123) he is given the opportunity to display his powers in many of the jobs available in the film capital of the world. It begins with a meeting between the movie star, Monica Malamar, and the executives of her company. Worried by the bad publicity she is getting by brawling in nightclubs, speeding in sports cars and continually getting divorced, they feel she needs a better image in order to play the lead in *Rebecca of Sunnybrook Farm*. Smitty, her press agent, arranges a personal appearance in Fort Baxter so that the newspapers can get some pictures of her surrounded by nice, clean-cut young soldiers.

The platoon go wild with the news, leaving Bilko to explain to them that the whole thing is a snow job.

'It burns me up to think that I have to play the wide-eyed innocent GI for Monica Malamar.'

'You, sarge?'

'Of course, they always pick one GI who gets the full treatment . . . the big hug and kiss, the cheek-to-cheek dancing, the champagne dinner! I suppose I'll have to go through with it.'

'What a noble sacrifice, sarge. Thanks for protecting us from all that ecstasy.'

Bilko gets himself chosen to pick up Monica Malamar; he suggests to Captain Barker that it might not be advisable for the captain to do it himself after what happened to Colonel . . . sorry, Private Wilson. Barker, aware how close he is to becoming a major, drafts Bilko to fetch her from her hotel in Grove City, despite Bilko's protests that he has a date that night with a very respectable librarian called Abigail.

At the hotel Bilko plays such a virtuoso performance as a wide-eyed, innocent GI that Smitty is struck with the idea of concocting a romance between the GI and the star. The newspapers would love it, Monica's reputation would zoom and they could dump him in a couple of weeks.

After a great night on the town, cruising round the restaurants and nightclubs of San Francisco in Monica's Jaguar, Bilko is congratulating himself the next day on a part well played. Smitty arrives, acting concerned, and tells him that last night was such a change for Monica. 'You're a clean-cut, wholesome guy – after all those bums she's known, you're a breath of fresh air.' He advises Bilko to stay out of her life, that her love for Bilko would affect her career. 'In particular, don't follow her to Hollywood. Don't haunt her apartment at Sunset Towers.'

Bilko is bowled over, Henshaw is sceptical: 'But, sarge, Monica Malamar and you, it doesn't make sense.'

'Did Romeo and Juliet make sense? Did the Duke of Windsor and Wally make sense? And what about Arthur Miller and Marilyn Monroe?'

Overwhelmed he rushes off to Hollywood just as Smitty planned and soon Louella Parsons is saying: 'We are all so happy that Monica has found Mr Right at last.'

Monica however is not so happy. Bilko is there all the time on set, in the dressing-room and in her apartment – and has the habit of kissing her on the neck. 'I don't want him slobbering over me any more. My neck is all chapped.'

At this point Bilko appears, the very image of a Hollywood character, and insists to the movie producer that the previous day's filming be done again, no expense spared. He also renegotiates her contract insisting on $400,000 a picture against 10 per cent of the gross profits. The producer asks Monica to tell Bilko where to get off – but to his surprise she kisses Bilko and insists that he becomes her agent. They sweep out to lunch leaving the producer and Smitty to brood on the Frankenstein they've created.

'In the last two weeks he's become an agent, a lawyer, a writer, a producer.'

'What's left?'

'A movie star!'

They decide to con him into a screen test, say it's great, dangle a fat contract in front of him and insist he give up Monica.

They arrange a chance meeting between Bilko and the celebrated film director, Emile Petroff, who has been primed to play his part. He is making a film of *The Three Musketeers* and says he is willing to pay $200,000 for the right man in the lead. Petroff does a double-take when he sees Bilko and claims that he has found his actor. Smitty pretends to protest: 'But Emile he doesn't even have hair.'

'What is Yul Brynner by you . . . a cocker spaniel?'

When Smitty says they don't know how he will photograph, Bilko produces a snapshot from his wallet: 'It was taken over two years ago . . . even then the virility comes through.'

A screen test is arranged and Smitty suggests that Bilko changes his name to Brick Bilko. The screen test goes well, or so Smitty tells Bilko, and he falls for the line that his career in movies will be jeopardized by his continued liaison with the scandal-prone Monica. When he tells Monica they're through, she laughs uproariously and points out what Smitty is doing.

Bilko hits himself on the forehead and exclaims: 'It shows you what vanity and conceit can do to a fine greedy mind like mine.'

Together they tell Smitty and the producer that they're getting married in Mexico that afternoon and Bilko forces them to sign the contract for $400,000 a picture. This done he and Monica say goodbye to each other and Bilko returns to Camp Fremont – unaware that Emile Petroff really does think his screen test was wonderful.

Bilko's forays into television are often as successful as his trips to Hollywood. After his attempt to turn Duane Doberman into a TV Western star his most impressive involvement with broadcasting came in 'Bilko's TV Idea' (Programme 55). Buddy Bickford, a TV comic of crashing awfulness, is plunging down through the ratings. His writers from the firm of Bigsby, Bigsby and Bigsby are cudgelling their brains for a new idea . . . and are struck by the idea of putting him in a situation comedy based on the army, set in a little post in the Mid-West. They arrange for Buddy to spend a week at Fort Baxter collecting material.

Sergeants Grover and Ritzik are overwhelmed by the news of his imminent arrival, the rest of the camp greets it with indifference or, in Bilko's case, suspicion. 'Why is Bickford suddenly coming to this camp? The last show that came through here was Vilma Banky and the turkey trot dancers. I'm suspicious when a comedian gets through with a TV season and doesn't go straight to a hospital like the rest of them do.'

Then he remembers Private Whitley was complaining that although he sent dozens of TV scripts to agencies none were ever accepted. Bilko guesses that one of them has been judged a success by Bigsby, Bigsby and Bigsby and that Bickford and his writers are on their way to buy the rights for a song. Determined that Whitley should get a good price for his idea (and that Bilko should get a good cut of it), Bilko becomes Whitley's agent.

The writers arrive and immediately Bilko sets to work. As soon as Colonel Hall is out of the room, Bilko starts in on the writers:

'Don't let this uniform fool you, boys. I have a connection with show business. I went to school with Bob Hope's cousin. We were on the wrestling team together. Lovely girl.'

He offers them the rights in Whitley's script 'Andrew Armstrong – Tree Surgeon' for $50,000.

At this point Colonel Hall re-enters: 'Gentlemen, has this sergeant been annoying you?'

'No.'

'That's strange. Ordinarily, left alone with two strangers, he would have sold you a Sherman tank.'

The writers then explain that they already have a TV idea, Buddy Bickford in the army, and they don't need to buy one from anybody.

Buddy arrives and immediately rubs everyone up the wrong way.

The colonel starts his welcome speech: 'Mr Bickford on behalf of the officers and men of –'

'Get this character. Funny. Remember that for the colonel of our show – a bumbler.'

Turning to Bilko, he starts: 'Who is this character? His head is shining in my eyes. You've got a beautiful head of skin there. It would make a fine skating rink for a midget. The last time I saw something like that I made it the hard way, in the side pocket.'

Mrs Hall arrives and Buddy is overjoyed: 'Boys, did you get that? Put her down. Colonel's wife, frumpy little chatterbox'.

Bilko broods in the barracks: 'They're at Fort Baxter. They're on my property, and when people are on my property they do what I want them to do and I want them to buy this script.'

He decides to break Buddy's confidence. The platoon are warned not to laugh at anything Buddy says. Buddy busts a gut trying to make them laugh and is plunged into gloom when they remain completely stone-faced. To boost his confidence the writers tell him about Ritzik and Grover: 'They laughed at your empty car when we showed it to them.'

Bilko sends Henshaw to take them to the sergeants' room by his 'shortcut', while he goes and primes Grover and Ritzik. He tells them that Buddy has one week to live and is hiding his doom behind a smile and a quip. Buddy arrives, the sergeants burst into tears and Bickford collapses calling for his analyst, his confidence completely shattered.

As he prepares to leave, Bilko approaches him and tells him that the new comedy craze is . . . wood. He says Bickford is out of touch with the public and that wood is cracking them up across the country. He gives Buddy the script of 'Andrew Armstrong – Tree Surgeon' and asks him to try it out on the (warned in advance) motor pool.

Mahogany, knotty pine, hickory, elm, maple . . . the platoon fall about the floor laughing. Buddy gets his confidence back. The writers are dubious and Buddy takes them to Grover and Ritzik. Bilko has been there first and told them that Buddy's life has been saved by a Dr Wood. He says that Buddy wants everyone to rejoice with him and to laugh at anything connected with wood. Buddy and the writers enter and fire off the names of trees, Grover and Ritzik collapse. Bilko tells them that a thousand dollars is enough: 'Wood belongs to the public. All we want is something for having called your attention to it.'

The writers' boss arrives and tells them that they are clean out of their minds and explains how Bilko has flim-flammed them into thinking wood is funny. As he does this, he realizes that Bilko is the character Buddy is looking for: 'a fenangling sergeant in the army, who can talk people into anything!'

Mr Bigsby is unimpressed: 'This Sergeant Bilko you think is the smartest, shrewdest operator in the army is one of the most stupid naive characters I've ever met. Who else would sell me the hottest property in years, "I married a chiropodist". Feet, they're laughing at feet!'

Bilko enters and asks for the money in cash and as Bigsby counts it out he cracks up with laughter as Bilko says: 'Arch, toenail, bunions . . .' Bilko leaves and all present realize that they, like so many others, have been taken for a ride by the sharpest master sergeant in the US Army.

The Greatest Bilko Ever – 'Bilko Gets Some Sleep'

*E*pisode 49 of The Phil Silvers Show 'You'll Never Get Rich' – otherwise known to the world as The Bilko Show – is called 'Bilko Gets Some Sleep'. We think it's just about the best there ever was. It may not have the belly-laugh appeal of the sight of a monkey on roller-skates which occurs in the wonderful 'The Court-Martial', nor the blissful crossed purposes that make 'Bilko Goes South' – in which the motor pool enter themselves for a deadly experiment in the belief that it is in fact a singing contest – so funny. But there are three good reasons for choosing it none the less.

Firstly the writing is magnificent throughout: Colonel Hall's rueful comments in the opening scenes, the desperate anxiety of the motor pool as their sarge goes straight, and the handling of the plot itself all show the writers (Nat Hiken, Tony Webster and Billy Friedberg) on top form. Then there is the archetypal quality of the story. It takes a familiar premise – that people always assume that Bilko is up to something even when he isn't – and extends it to the nth degree. Anyone who cares to read deeply, or even pretentiously into comedy might be interested in the way that Bilko is seen to be taking care of all the collected neuroses of the entire camp; when he stops being crazy everyone else starts, when he starts to sleep easy everyone else becomes an insomniac. Unlikely as it may sound, he is the scapegoat of Fort Baxter. And lastly there is Bilko's astonishing and entirely ad-libbed speech to his psychiatrist, which is Phil Silvers' single greatest comic tour de force.

The story opens one morning with the news that Bilko is, as always, late with the morning report from the motor pool. Joan, however, is defending him to the other WACs because she

Phil Silvers as himself ...

... and as miracle medico extraordinary ('Bilko's Formula 7') ...

... a smart San Francisco Butler ('Bilko the Butler') ...

... Chief Bald Eagle ('Cherokee Ernie') ...

... a Hollywood
movie producer
('The Colonel's
Second
Honeymoon') ...

... a jailed Mexican bandito ('Viva Bilko') ...

... and a pukka English army officer ('Bilko's Credit Card') ...

happens to know, since Ernie cancelled their date, that he was in mourning for his Uncle Felix all night. When the other girls are sceptical she insists, 'I know when Ernie's lying and when he's telling the truth. When he tells the truth he always looks like he's in great pain. You should have seen him last night . . . Mary, it's terrible to see a grown man cry.'

Colonel Hall, however, is less easily convinced: 'His uncle? You mean he still had one left? If he'd just send something in one paper . . . just a little hint that his platoon is still with us.'

Joan leaps to Bilko's defence: 'Really colonel, I realize Sergeant Bilko is a little behind on his reports . . .'

'A *little* behind? Bilko hasn't even reported Pearl Harbor yet. Send for my jeep. Mrs Hall and I are going into town.'

'I'm sorry, sir,' says Joan, 'Sergeant Bilko said your jeep is still being given its five-thousand-mile check.'

'Every time I want my jeep he's giving it a check. If we ever go into battle I'll be the only commanding officer who has to lead his troops in a taxi cab. When you see him tell him I want to have a talk with him.'

'I'll call him immediately.'

'Oh, don't wake him up just for that. It's only eleven o'clock.'

'Sir, don't be too hard.'

'Oh no. I just want to clear up a misconception in his mind. I want to explain that he joined the army, not a retirement plan.'

The colonel leaves Joan's office, but Ritzik and Grover enter, chatting about their all-night poker game with Bilko. When Ernie himself arrives on the scene Joan is not to be dissuaded by any of his feeble excuses and storms out with the announcement that she never wants to see him again. Bilko moves on to Colonel Hall's office, where the colonel is just ordering a cab to take him into town with his wife.

'Why, Sergeant Bilko, what are you doing here so early?' asks the colonel. 'Did the sound of honest soldiers working wake you up? Bilko, I've reached a big decision. I've decided to relieve you of the command of this post and take over myself.'

Bilko decides on diversionary tactics and turns to Mrs Hall. 'I don't believe we've had the pleasure.'

'Oh come, Sergeant Bilko,' she giggles.

'Colonel Hall, no one told me one of the major film companies was on location here at Fort Baxter. Would you introduce me to Miss Taylor or are you already calling her Elizabeth? Why, it's Mrs Hall. If you get any younger we'll lose you to Elvis Presley.'

The colonel pleads for quiet, but Bilko is undeterred: 'There's a rock 'n' roll party in town Saturday. See you there with the other

41

kids?'

'If you can spare the time,' insists the colonel, 'I'd like to discuss some military matters with you.'

To wit, the matters of the morning reports and the colonel's jeep. Bilko does his best to distract attention from the subjects in hand ('Has the resemblance between Napoleon and your husband struck you? You remember Napoleon . . . What am I saying? He was before your time.') but the colonel gets to the point in the end: 'You've had my jeep in your shop for the past three weeks. Why?'

'Sir, would you mind telling me your age?'

'What has my age got to do with the fact that I never see my jeep?'

'Only this, sir,' explains Bilko, 'You have the legs of a man in his twenties . . . legs of steel and yet with the spring of a young panther. And why? Because you do more walking than any other colonel in the United States Army.'

Colonel Hall is not impressed and insists that until Bilko's reports are up to date and his own jeep fixed the sergeant may not use any military vehicles. So Bilko picks up the colonel's taxi on his way out. Meanwhile Colonel Hall has another matter with which to deal. Captain Adams, the base psychiatrist, is leaving the following day because he has no work to do: 'I've never seen a better mentally adjusted group of men than you have here, colonel.'

'Thank you,' says Colonel Hall. 'I suppose healthy bodies make healthy minds. I personally do a great deal of walking.' He then looks out of his window, sees that his cab has been taken and yells after the departing Bilko, 'I'll kill him! I'll kill him!'

The shrink is impressed: 'That's why this is such a well-adjusted post, there are no frustrations.'

The scene then shifts forward to Bilko's room that night. The boys are playing poker, but there's only been a dime on the table all evening and come ten o'clock everyone is off to bed, despite Bilko's attempts to keep the game going. 'That wasn't poker, that was seven-handed solitaire,' he tells his loyal henchmen Henshaw and Barbella.

Not even they, however, are prepared to stay up late and they leave him alone to try to get some sleep. He can't do it and starts pacing round his room. Suddenly he hears a voice coming from a figure that looks like a milder version of himself: same bald patch and glasses, but less swagger. This is his conscience: 'I'm probably the smallest and most ignored conscience in the English-speaking people, but I'm still your conscience.'

The conscience knows why Bilko can't sleep – he has too much guilt on his mind. He's been taking advantage of the colonel, for example.

'Taking advantage of the colonel? Show me one case where I haven't treated him as an equal,' Bilko demands.

But there is more to come. He's been bad to Joan, too, stringing her along for five years without marrying her. And then there's the platoon; honest, hard-working soldiers and all he can do is connive and scheme against them. He should become an honest human being again.

Just when Bilko is about to take this advice another character appears – flash and smarmy with a leopardskin dressing gown and a cigarette holder. This is Bilko's ego. As far as he's concerned the conscience is just a square. But he thinks that the way that Bilko is handling the colonel and Joan is just fine, although he reckons Bilko can do better: 'There's a hot hunk of stuff dancing at the Latin Quarter. I'm working on her for you. It'll take a little money, but I got some real slick gimmicks that'll shake it loose from that platoon of yours.'

His conscience and his ego continue to torment Ernie until he cries out, 'Leave me alone! I don't know what to do! All I know is I can't sleep. Leave me alone. Leave me alone.'

Rocco and Henshaw, alarmed by the noise, charge back into Bilko's room, only to find him screaming to himself. They shake him loose from his dream and he begs them to stay and talk to him. They say they can't. They have a big day tomorrow. They've got to help move Captain Adams off the post. No wonder he's leaving – who'd ever want to go and see him. Bilko agrees – you'd have to have your head examined if you wanted to do a thing like that. But he does arrange to come along and help them – just for the exercise.

The following morning sees Bilko in Captain Adams' office engaging him in conversation while Rocco and Henshaw move the furniture – except for the couch, which Bilko insists they leave behind. The sarge tells the psychiatrist that a friend of his is having trouble sleeping and keeps hearing voices which keep him up night after night. Perhaps, says the psychiatrist, perhaps this fellow has guilt problems. Bilko agrees that this might be the case, but points out that the man is one of the gentlest and most sensitive . . .

'Sergeant,' interrupts Captain Adams, 'This friend of yours who can't sleep – is he a master sergeant? Does he wear glasses?'

Bilko feigns amazement: 'You mean, is it . . .? Oh no, I'm as normal as blueberry pie. Why – I'm the last person in the world who . . .' Suddenly he breaks down and flings himself sobbing onto the couch: 'I need help!'

'Now, now sergeant, tell me what's troubling you.'

And then the soliloquy begins: 'Don't ask me. Ask the whole post. They're all against me. The colonel thinks I'm always goofing off work and my girl . . . there's a case for you. She thinks everything I say is a lie. For five years she's been stringing me along. I don't think she wants to get married at all. I'm a homebody really. And my platoon – I offer them my affection and what do they do? They reject me. They walk all over me. They take advantage of my father complex. Don't you see what it is? It's the id complex versus the libido, sir. When they're rejecting me it's not me they're rejecting but a dream image. Freud said it in his thesis about the male anima and its rejection of the male image. I don't have to tell you about that, sir, you know all about it. It all came out in Freud's debate with Spinoza many years ago in Budapest in which he presented the theory that destroyed Schopenhauer's theory of the Oedipus complex. Spinoza himself, as a devoted disciple of Schopenhauer's screamed at Freud, "Sigmund, you're insane!" Freud came right back and said, "Barry, listen to me. I know what I'm saying." And Freud came right back with his theory, which he maintained. He told them about sadism and inner masochism. You can see it in Joan – an inner masochism. She denies everything I say. She knows it's the truth, but in her rejections she reverts to masochism and denies everything I say. Why? It's a rejection of me. I don't know where it came from, sir. Maybe before she was born her mother hated glasses. I don't know, sir, but Freud said it. Freud came out with the theory of the id complex and its manifestation in rejection theory. It's a bedlam of guilt. You see it on the post with the colonel and the men. The colonel salutes. The men salute. Salute . . . salute . . . what is that salute, sir? It's a symbol of insecurity. Don't you see what it says in essence? "Love me, I love you. Want me, I want you." Don't you see, sir – it's an inner bedlam of conflict. The id complex versus the alter-ego. The manifestation of the theory of the hedriogentian cycle. It's as plain as the nose on my face. I see it. Why can't I sleep?'

The psychiatrist tries to get Bilko to tell him the truth about the life he leads at Fort Baxter. 'Truth is the foundation of analysis. Telling the truth is much better than lying.'

'Sir, that's open to honest debate.'

'Sergeant Bilko! And you wonder why you can't sleep, when your brain is so busy thinking up schemes, filled with guilt about the lies you've been telling, the people you've mistreated. Tell me, how do you get along with your fellow men?'

'Oh, they love me. Why, only the other day . . .'

'The truth, Bilko.'

'They hate me.'

'And this girl, who's been stringing you along?'

'She hates me.'

'And the colonel?'

'He hates me.'

'Bilko, tell me everything.'

'You hate me. Everybody hates me.'

'Is there any wonder, with your lying, conniving and disregarding military regulations?'

'What can I do?'

'You're a soldier. Start living as a soldier. Get up with your men in the morning, do your work, be a useful member of the post . . . someone people can love instead of hate.'

'Love? Will they really love me?'

'If you just give them a chance. Tell the truth. Earn their respect.'

And so a new Bilko is born and Captain Adams phones his wife to tell her to stop packing. Clearly they are going to be needed for a long time to come.

The scene shifts once more: the following morning in the motor pool's washroom. The men are washing and grumbling amongst themselves when in comes Bilko, bright as a button. Nobody notices him as he marches into the showers. Suddenly all the other showers stop and bemused soldiers emerge: 'I don't believe it,' says Kadowski.

'It was him, it was him!' cries Sugy.

'Yeah, it was Bilko. He's up! He's up!'

They gaze over the partition into the shower where Bilko is singing loudly, 'For it's hi, hi, he in the Field Artillery. . .'

Mullen walks into the washroom: 'Will you shut up in there? You'll wake Bilko. That's a ten dollar fine.'

Bilko walks out of the shower as his men do a double-take. Yes, it really is him. Rocco and Henshaw come in and start to escort Bilko from the room; it's fine, they say, he's only sleepwalking. No, say Bilko, he's up and awake. Oh, replies Henshaw, he must have had a hard night and is just freshening up before retiring to bed. But Bilko pooh-poohs the fuss: 'I'm a soldier. A soldier gets up at six o'clock. I'm up.' He wipes some shaving foam off Doberman's ear. Straightens Paparelli's tie. 'What's everybody staring at me for?'

'Well,' says Paparelli, 'It's just that you're up like everybody else.'

'That's right,' replies Bilko. 'We're all human beings, aren't we?'

'*We're* human beings, yeah. But we've come to think of *you* as some sort of a sun god.'

'Well, that's all part of the past,' concludes the sarge. 'We're gonna do things together from now on. I'm gonna be right by your side in the motor pool. This is the way to live. Giving the army an honest day's work for a day's pay. Take your time, fellas, I gotta make out my morning report.'

The men are stunned.

Mullen: 'What's he up to?'

Zimmerman: 'He's up to something.'

Paparelli: 'But what? What?'

Mullen: 'Boys, we're in trouble.'

Doberman: 'I thought he was very sweet.'

Paparelli: 'Jerk! He's softening us up for something.'

Finally Fender comes up with an answer: 'Boys, I think what we've been afraid of for the last couple of years is finally going to happen . . . he's going to sell us into slavery.'

At the colonel's office there are more surprises in store. Joan is amazed to see Bilko bring in his report. 'What's so strange?' retorts Bilko. 'A sergeant brings in a morning report. What do you think the army pays me for?'

'I don't know,' concedes Joan. 'I thought maybe you had something on the Chief of Staff.'

But there's more to come. Bilko suggests they 'investigate this funny little old American custom called marriage.' Ritzik's married. Why don't the two of them go over to the Ritziks' house and just see how they like it?

'I knew it!' cries Joan. 'You won Ritzik's house from him in a poker game. Ernie, they have a child!'

'Joan, I won nothing but my self-respect. And now that I've won that there's only one more thing I want to win . . . you.'

Joan is left dumbfounded as Bilko marches in to see the colonel. 'Oh, Bilko,' says the commandant. 'I didn't realize it was that late. Time for lunch, huh?' Bilko explains that it is in fact 7.30. No, not 7.30 p.m., but 7.30 a.m. and that he has some motor pool requisitions for the colonel to sign. Colonel Hall looks as though he is in a state of shock: 'I'll be all right. I just need a little time to think this over.'

Bilko moves on to the colonel's jeep. He's afraid that they haven't finished working on it. The colonel is relieved: 'Good, good. I was beginning to think the whole world was going crazy.'

'However, sir,' says Bilko, 'Your command car is all ready for you.'

'I *have* a command car?'

'Army regulations give every colonel a command car,' Bilko assures him.

'They do? What does it look like?'

'It's very attractive. It's a khaki four-door sedan.'

'Oh, *that* car. I thought it belonged to you.'

'Oh no. It came in six months ago. I was just checking it, sir, to make sure it was road safe. After driving it for eight thousand miles I now feel that it's safe enough for my commanding officer.'

'Oh, thank you.'

Bilko moves to the window. 'There it is, sir. It's a beauty.'

The colonel, however, is looking at Bilko, rather than the car. 'It's amazing,' he says. 'This is the first time I've ever seen you in the sunlight. I've always thought you were a much shorter man.'

Bilko assures him that he'll be around in the daytime from now on and hurries off to get some rifle practice, leaving Colonel Hall perplexed: 'What's he up to? Why did he do it? Why? Why?'

Joan is equally puzzled. She calls her mother to see if any relatives have died and left her a lot of money. 'Think!' she pleads. 'I don't care how distant the relative . . . Bilko would know before we did.' But none have died, and she too is left wondering.

The colonel emerges and asks if she has noticed anything odd about Bilko. They agree that something's up. Then Nell Hall arrives, dying to take a spin in the new command car. The colonel forbids her to touch it and calls Lieutenant Samuels to send over a demolition man: 'I think there's a bomb planted in my command car. I want him to take that car apart – every single part has to be gone over. We're dealing with a desperate man!'

Mrs Hall is appalled, but her husband is certain: 'I was very hard with him yesterday. I knew he'd try to get even . . . but murder!' He begs Sergeant Hogan to be a witness. Now she knows why Bilko wants to marry her – a wife can't testify against her husband.

By now Bilko is seeing the chaplain and offering to help with the annual chapel bazaar. He'll bake cakes, put up bunting, build the booths, anything to be of assistance: 'I have a feeling that if the bazaar is a success, I'll be a success.'

The chaplain's reaction is immediate. As soon as Bilko leaves his office he picks up a phone: 'Sergeant Dugan, the annual chapel bazaar is called off until further notice. That's right, and check the poor box.'

Over in Bilko's room, Rocco and Henshaw are pacing back and forth. They can't figure out what's happening. Everyone on the post is tense, fights are breaking out, but Bilko just glides around with a big smile on his face. Just then the man himself comes in, wearing his pyjamas and ready for bed. It's nine o'clock and he has a twenty-mile hike the next day. He yawns, gets into bed and promptly falls fast asleep, wreathed in smiles.

'He knows something, he knows something,' says Henshaw and begs Rocco for a cigarette. They head off to the latrine to smoke it only to find the whole platoon there, pacing round and around. None of them can sleep. They're desperate: 'Let's put all the money we've got, every dime, and leave it in front of his door. Maybe he'll take pity,' suggests Mullen.

Fender is still convinced they've all been sold. Then Doberman appears in full battle-dress with a pack on his back: 'I'm going over the wall,' he says.

'You can't go AWOL,' says Mullen.

'Let me go!' pleads Doberman. 'I don't want to be here when it happens.'

But when *what* happens? They start to pace again.

Colonel Hall is equally tense, walking around his bedroom as his wife sits up in bed.

'It wasn't in the command car. Where could he have put it? I looked everywhere.'

'John, go to bed!' commands his wife.

'The bed!' exclaims the colonel, and dives underneath it in search of bombs.

Three days later Bilko turns up at Dr Adams' office. But he can't get into see the psychiatrist without an appointment. He must wait like everyone else. A phone rings and Dr Adams' secretary answers: 'Oh no, not a chance. A week from today? I'll check and call you back.'

The doctor's office door opens and the colonel emerges: 'Colonel, you must get some sleep.'

'Sleep, sleep . . .'

'It's just a persecution complex. No one wants to kill you.'

But the colonel is not certain: 'It's terrible. Yesterday at assembly when they sang the Star-Spangled Banner, when they came to the part about "bombs bursting in the air" . . . I ducked.'

Then Joan comes in to see the analyst. She too emerges with comforting words from Dr Adams: 'Just because a man gets up at six o'clock in the morning and proposes marriage is no reason to . . .'

In comes Mrs Hall, complaining that her husband makes her test the soup for poison before he'll drink it. When she emerges the entire motor pool replace her. They have group insomnia. When they come out the doctor is asking, 'Because your sergeant is nice to you, does things for you, is concerned for your welfare, is that any reason to be afraid?' Their answer is unanimous – yes!

Bilko has been hiding behind a newspaper all this while. Adams spots him: 'Bilko, what have you been doing to this post?'

'All I'm doing is finally getting a good night's sleep.'

'But nobody else is. I need help.'

So saying, Adams disappears into his office. Bilko turns to his men. There are going to be a few changes. They'll go ahead with the rifle practice, but it'll be three shots for a quarter: 'Henshaw – got the kewpie dolls?' And there's a new schedule. Anyone waking him before noon will be fined twenty-five bucks.

'You can't do this,' complain the soldiers. 'We're free men.'

But Bilko assures them, 'I'll do whatever I want to do.'

Adams re-emerges to fix the platoon's next appointment, but it won't be necessary. They'll be back to sleeping like babies.

The colonel reappears, certain that he knows where the bomb is. Bilko promptly announces that he's taken the staff car back for repairs and he has to check it; how fast it will go, how many girls it will hold. An argument ensues and Adams is worried for his patient: 'Colonel, colonel, you're upsetting yourself.'

'Upsetting myself? I never felt better in my life. Bilko I'm going to have a talk with you. Once and for all we're going to settle who runs this base.'

So saying he leaves. Now only Joan remains to be cured. Bilko simply takes back his proposal: 'Have you got it in writing? Have you got witnesses? Anyway I'm in mourning for my uncle.'

'Ernie, you're lying!'

'Honey, I could never lie to you. You know you're the only girl in the world for me.'

They kiss and Joan departs contented. Everything has returned to normal. Bilko has returned to his wicked ways, everyone knows just where they stand again and the psychiatrist can leave the base. But even if Bilko's conscience is appeased, his ego still has unfinished business: 'She's called Zsa-Zsa L'Amour. Now, she expects you tonight at the Silver Palace. Here's what you've got to do . . .'

A Bilko A–Z

A

ABERNETHY, Coach. Also known as 'The Fox'. Aged football coach at Schmill University (qv), whom Bilko persuades to communicate with press only via nods, smiles and winks, thereby driving reporters into a frenzy of speculation on the true strength of the Schmill team. Ref. 'Bilko Goes to College' – Programme 37.

ADAMS, Dr/Capt. Psychiatrist about to leave Fort Baxter due to lack of patients until Bilko seeks his advice. (See 'The Greatest Bilko Ever'.) Ref. 'Bilko Gets Some Sleep' – Programme 49.

ALDA, Alan. Superstar actor and male feminist best-known for role as Hawkeye in M*A*S*H, but appears to Bilko as Carlisle Thompson (qv), 24-year-old heir to shipping magnate in New York. Ref. 'Bilko The Art Lover' – Programme 94.

ALTOONA. Pennsylvanian community that is Duane Doberman's home town, where Bilko and others are held hostage by robbers while staying with Duane's mother en route to New York. Ref. 'Bilko at Bay' – Programme 86.

ANDERSON, Lt. Played by Jim Perry. Fresh-faced member of the Fort Baxter officer corps who appears throughout 1st series but never subsequently. No distinguishing characteristics.

ARMSTRONG, Andrew, Tree Surgeon. Central character of Pvt. Whitley's would-be TV series of same name, which Bilko tries to sell to Buddy Bickford (qv). Ref. 'Bilko's TV Idea' – Programme 55.

B

BARBELLA, Angie. Brother of Rocco (qv); is engaged to marry Italian peasant girl called Rosa (qv), but feels that she is not good enough for him. Ref. 'The Girl From Italy' – Programme 41.

BARBELLA, Cpl. Rocco. Played by Hervey Lembeck. Along with Cpl. Henshaw (qv) is Bilko's devoted sidekick and fundraiser from the first episode – in which Bilko manages to lose $100 of his money to Sgt. Sowici *et al* in a fixed poker game – to the last – in which he, Bilko and Henshaw end up in the guardhouse for good. Tends to be the more credulous of the two corporals.

BARBER, Red. Famed American sports writer who meets Bilko when Hank Lumpkin (qv) joins the platoon. Ref. 'Hillbilly Whiz' – Programme 79.

BARKER, Capt. Played by Nick Saunders. Second in command to Col. Hall at Fort Baxter and Camp Fremont. Is Hall's lone ally and consequently the butt of much Bilko-inspired activity. Briefly busted down to Lieutenant after the Harry Speakup affair (qv). Otherwise undistinguished.

BAYCHER, Sgt. Takes over from Bilko as head of the motor pool after Bilko gets himself transferred. Drives Col. Hall mad by being super-efficient and loading him up with work never created by Bilko. Ref. 'Transfer' – Programme 22.

BELLBOY. Horse bought and taken to barracks by Bilko and his men in the hope that it can be trained into Triple Crown-winning racehorse. Ref. 'The Horse' – Programme 3.

BELLMAN, Roger. Millionaire Detroit auto-manufacturer with whom Bilko stays (surrounded by luscious beauties) whilst trying to persuade him to buy do-it-yourself car kits. Ref. 'Bilko F.O.B. Detroit' – Programme 74.

BENSON, Sgt. Quentin B. 'The Beast'. Super-tough drill sergeant brought to Fort Baxter by Col. Hall in the hope of turning Bilko and co. into decent soldiers. Is unnerved when Bilko takes out $100,000 insurance policy on him with Bilko, Rocco and Henshaw as beneficiaries. Ref. 'Bilko and the Beast' – Programme 31.

BERRA, Yogi. One of the all-time great baseball players. Meets Bilko in Hank Lumpkin episode. Ref. 'Hillbilly Whiz' – Programme 79.

BICKFORD, Buddy. Fading comedian. Catch-phrase; 'I doody-deedy-do!' Ref. 'Bilko's TV Idea' – Programme 55.

BIGBSY, BIGBSY & BIGBSY. Advertising agency that sponsors Buddy Bickford (qv). Ref. 'Bilko's TV Idea' – Programme 55.

BILKO, Brick. Name given to Ernie when picked by Emile Petroff (qv) as a potential Hollywood star. Ref. 'Bilko's Hollywood Romance' – Programme 123.

BILKO, Clem. Quick-witted younger brother of Swifty Bilko (qv) and cousin of Ernie (qv). Briefly seen when he wanders into motor pool following his brother's departure, takes off cap to reveal eyeshade and sits right down to a game of poker. Ref. 'Bilko's Cousin' – Programme 85.

BILKO, M/Sgt. Ernest G. (RA 15042699). Played by Phil Silvers. Fenangling, scheming, quick-witted master sergeant. Joined army in 1941 and served in China, New Guinea, Marianas Island, Kabuchi Island, Saipan and France. Commissioned as temporary Lieutenant in 1943 during action in the Marianas. Order not rescinded until 1957 ('Lieutenant Bilko' – Programme 84) although Bilko decides not to insist his commission is honoured upon discovering that back pay in excess of $20,000 is exceeded by dues paid for food, clothing etc by officers. Obsessed by gambling and showbiz. Endlessly trying to raise money. Finally ends up in guardhouse. See all preceding/subsequent chapters in this book.

BILKO, Felix. Imaginary uncle of Ernest Bilko, who uses his equally imaginary demise as an excuse for not seeing Joan. Ref. 'Bilko Gets Some Sleep' – Programme 49.

BILKO, Major Joshua. Ancestor of Bilko, the discovery of his diary persuades Bilko to apply for officer training in honour of his family's military traditions. Reads Journal and discovers that tradition of conmanship more consistent than that of soldiering. In winter of 1777, while American Revolutionary Army under Gen. Washington cold and starving at camp at Valley Forge, Maj. Bilko remains plump and prosperous organizing turkey raffles for the troops, which he always wins. Pulls out enormous turkey leg in front of Washington and General Staff, none of whom have eaten for three days. Says: 'General, I wish you could have been there to see the eyes of our men, those gallant men in their tattered rags as they looked up at me as I drew the lucky number. Oh, it almost made me cry.' General Washington: 'Before those starving men you had the audacity to take the turkey?' Bilko: 'Good heavens, General. I won it, didn't I?' 'But as an officer you had an opportunity to make a beautiful gesture.' 'Oh, by Jove I did – I let them watch as I ate the drumstick – they were overwhelmed. I had to whip some of them, "Down!" I said, "Get down!" ' Enter Mrs Washington and the Bilko silver tongue goes to work once more: 'The sun shines again and it is spring at Valley Forge. General, you didn't tell me you had engaged this young actress to entertain the troops. Well, good heavens, it's Mrs Washington. If you get any younger the men will revolt.' Discusses decoration of the officers' club ('I think we'll do the billiard room in Chippendale') with Mrs W. while the general is trying to conduct a stategy meeting. Persuades Washington to cross the River Brandywine – thereby changing whole course of Revolutionary War – because he has a date with two barmaids there. Behaviour continues to be appalling. Modern Bilko decides not to join officer corps after all. Ref. 'Revolutionary War' – Programme 19.

BILKO, Minerva. Great-aunt of Ernest who sends him diaries of Maj. Joshua Bilko (qv). Ref. 'Revolutionary War' – Programme 19.

BILKO, Swifty. Played by Dick Van Dyke. Country cousin of Ernest, who hopes that he will follow in the Bilko tradition, but is sadly disappointed. Sits down to game of poker and wins by bluffing Grover into throwing away a good hand when he only has a pair of twos by simple process of repeating everything he says, raising and raising the stakes until Grover drops out. On next hand Swifty throws away three aces. Admits he has never played cards before. Then allows Doberman to sell him a rifle. Bilko despairs and has Swifty posted to Mt. Washington. Ref. 'Bilko's Cousin' – Programme 85.

BILLINGS, Mr. Tax-evader whose records become mixed with those of Bilko, thereby initiating an IRS investigation into all his army rackets. Ref. 'Bilko's Tax Trouble' – Programme 46.

BOUDEREAU, M. et Mme. Roseville restaurateurs whose Casserole Boudereau is a delicious recipe, which Bilko wishes to steal for a cooking competition. They refuse to give it to him under any circumstances. Bilko even tries to force it out of their son by bribery and then force ('I'm a peace-loving man and I hate to say this, but sometimes you have to resort to violence') but is foiled by son's friend ('You're a big boy. Why don't you go and play with the traffic'). Ref. 'The Mess Hall Mess' – Programme 61.

BROWN SUEDE COMBAT BOOTS. Song written by Bilko for

Elvin Pelvin (qv), which runs, 'I gotta stand inspection/Before they let me leave/If I fail that ol' inspection/Tear the stripes off my sleeves/But don't you tread on my brown suede combat boots. I know I gotta drill/I know I gotta fight/Wake me up every morning by the dawn's early light/But don't you tread on my brown suede combat boots.' Ref. 'Rock'n'Roll Rookie' – Programme 57.

BRUBAKER, Pvt. New recruit whose perfect tenor voice ruins Bilko's plan to win a fortune by betting against his own platoon in a singing contest. Ref. 'The Singing Contest' – Programme 9.

C

CAMP FREMONT. Entirely undistinguished abandoned old army camp outside Grove City, California (qv), which Bilko believes lies on top of an old gold mine which he has discovered on a map drawn on the back of an old painting. Cannot mention gold in front of other men, so refers to it as 'potatoes', as in: 'There's potatoes in them thar hills'. Gets to California to discover that a highway is about to be built through the site of the old camp, so starts a campaign via army veterans to get Camp Fremont reopened. Not only that, has all the units from Fort Baxter posted there. Eventually discovers that The Gold Mine is an abandoned saloon. In disgust sells the painting on which the map is drawn for $40. It is in fact by the American master painter Remington and is worth $5000. It is, however, too late for the men to move back to Fort Baxter and they stay at Camp Fremont for the rest of the final series. Ref. 'Gold Fever' – Programme 108 and subsequent episodes.

CHADWICK, C. D. Also known as 'Hokey-Pokey' Chadwick. Hollywood film mogul who hires Bilko as military adviser to latest production (See also MUNDANE, Rory and GLOW, Gloria). Expects him to do nothing ('I don't like soldiers around when I'm making a war movie') but discovers that he is not like other soldiers; 'C. D. – I think your films are wonderful. They used to show your battle pictures whenever there was a lull in the fighting. They used to take our minds off the war. Maybe the critics don't like them, but they're dogs, mad dogs. I'm not going to tell you how to make pictures. I wouldn't presume. I'm just going to sit here quiet as a mouse.' Does exact opposite and drives Chadwick crazy. After a week there have been sixty-seven takes of first scene and nothing else, principally due to Bilko's refusal to accept any of Chadwick's proposals for the role of himself: 'It was easier to cast *Gone With the Wind*,' complains the producer. Eventually throws Bilko off the set and closes the picture. Writes damning report on Bilko to Col. Hall, but Pentagon – who hate Chadwick's pictures – delighted and a general calls to congratulate Bilko personally. Ref. 'Bilko in Hollywood' – Programme 17.

CHICKERING, Greg. A former soldier buddy of Bilko's, whom he tries to help towards his inheritance with a plot that is a parody of that for *The Maltese Falcon*. Ref. 'Where There's A Will' – Programme 45.

CLARA. Played by Fifties star Gretchen Wyler. Raucous Miami barmaid who becomes Bilko's 'bride' after he has gone on 'honeymoon' to Florida with Paparelli in drag and meets Col. and Mrs Hall. Ref. 'Bilko's Honeymoon' – Programme 98.

CLUSTERMAN, Charlie. Short-order cook who is the colonel's doppelganger. Persuaded by Bilko to imitate Col. Hall with disastrous consequences. (See 'Bilko And The Colonel'.) Ref. 'Weekend Colonel' – Programme 142.

COLBY, Congressman. One of three congressmen who visit Fort Baxter during an investigation into army waste, only to find that Bilko has painted a picture of abject misery; men with no boots receiving food parcels from Europe, etc. Ref. 'The Big Investigation' – Programme 16.

COLLINGSWORTH III, George. Rich man who buys flock of Fort Baxter carrier pigeons from Bilko, who has trained them to be racing pigeons, as a result of which they all fly straight back to Fort Baxter. Ref. 'Bilko's Pigeons – Programme 87.

COVINGTON, J. J. Ultra-sharp sergeant who threatens Bilko's domination and even persuades Bilko to buy 30,000 tons of entirely useless Japanese volcanic ash. Ref. 'Bilko vs. Covington' – Programme 110.

CROSBY, Bing. Crosby in person appears at Fort Baxter after Bilko has persuaded him to star in a show for the troops. Is late arriving, forcing Bilko to put on a lookalike. Just as the men are about to become angry the real Bing arrives, but instead of singing proceeds to recite 'The Wreck of the Hesperus'. There is also a non-syndicated Bilko show called 'The Bilkos and the Crosbys' in which Bilko fantasizes about how life would be if he, and not Bing, were the father of the Crosby family. Main Ref. 'Bilko Presents Bing Crosby' – Programme 52.

CUNNINGHAM, Deborah. Daughter of San Franciscan magnate, with whose butler Bilko lunches in the hope of meeting and marrying an heiress. Hears that Deborah is coming downstairs to kitchen for tea: 'That's the kind of heiress I admire, not too class-conscious.' Unfortunately she is only ten and a rude brat; 'I came to dinner eleven years too soon.' Ref. 'Bilko The Butler' – Programme 134.

D

DARCEL, Dixie. Striptease dancer who agrees to be married to Doberman when he appears to be the heir to a fortune. Ref. 'Doberman, Missing Heir' – Programme 137.

DE WITT, Franklin. Investment banker who soldiers with the National Guard. Bilko tries to persuade him to invest in a seedy night club. Ref. 'Bilko Buys a Club' – Programme 78.

DILLINGHAM, Pvt. Claude. Played by Walter Cartier. Regular member of the motor pool most noticeable for the fact that he is one of the very few members of Bilko's platoon who actually looks like the ideal of a handsome soldier. Springs to prominence when it is discovered that he is an ex-Golden Gloves boxing champion. It is, however, hard to get him angry enough to fight, as Bilko soon discovers. Ref. 'The Boxer' – Programme 20.

DIMMELDORF LODGE. Holiday resort at which Bilko, the motor pool and the Halls all find themselves simultaneously. Ref. 'Bilko's Vacation' – Programme 103.

DOBERMAN, Diane. Twin-sister of Duane (qv), who, Bilko tries to persuade the platoon, is a raving beauty; sadly, she is not. Ref. 'Doberman's Sister' – Programme 44.

DOBERMAN, Pvt. Duane. Played by Maurice Gosfield. War veteran, quiz genius, occasional cowboy, prince and socialite, stand-in spaceman and spark-plug and sometime broadcaster. This rotund super-slob is second only to Bilko in the Fort Baxter pantheon and went on to even greater heights of cool when transformed into Benny the Ball in the Top Cat cartoon series. (See 'Duane Doberman – Portrait of a Legend' and MOTOR POOL.)

DOBERMAN, Tex. Cowboy alter-ego of Duane (qv). Stars in pilot of own TV show after being spotted by CBS TV moguls.

Theme song runs: 'Who made Billy the Kid turn and run/Who shot Johnny Ringo just for fun/Who taught Wyatt Earp how to use a gun/Doberman – Tex Doberman. When they found Jesse James pumped full of lead/They said, "Name your killer before you're dead"/With his last breath Jesse sighed and said/"Doberman – Tex Doberman".' Ref. 'Bilko's TV Pilot' – Programme 100.

DRAYLIN, Paul. Real-life card expert imported by Col. Hall to ensure that Ritzik and co. beat Bilko at cards, thereby forcing him to retire from gambling. Ref. 'Bilko Retires From Gambling' – Programme 102.

E

EAGLE, Bald. Indian name given to Sgt. Bilko in his attempt to help Cpl. Charlie Whiteagle's family regain the water-rights to their ranch. On the discovery of an apparently invalidated treaty rolled up inside a peace-pipe, it turns into his campaign as leader of the entire Cherokee nation to have Oklahoma given back to the Indians. Ref. 'Cherokee Ernie' – Programme 81.

F

FELICIA. Girlfriend of Pvt. Claude Dillingham (qv). Ref. 'The Boxer' – Programme 20.

FENDER, Pvt. Sam. Played by Herbie Faye. Small, balding, middle-aged member of the motor pool bowed down by pessimism (he always believes the worst of Bilko: in 'Bilko Gets Some Sleep' he is the one who believes that the sarge has sold the platoon into slavery) and by his loathing of his wife and six children. (See MOTOR POOL.)

FLEISCHMAN, Pvt. Played by Maurice Brenner. Bespectacled, ugly and of no individual importance. (See MOTOR POOL.)

FORBES, Pvt. Former physical training teacher, whom Bilko wishes to lauch as a potential Mr Universe and subsequently a film star. Wrestles with 'gorilla' Doberman with disastrous results. Ref. 'Bilko's Ape Man' – Programme 131.

FORMULA 7. Miracle skincare cream made from applejack and crankcase oil, which Bilko tries to sell to cosmetics millionairess Deborah Darling. Ref. 'Bilko's Formula 7' – Programme 129.

FORTRIGHT, Congressman. Another of the visiting congressmen investigating waste at Fort Baxter (see COLBY, Congressman). Ref. 'The Big Investigation' – Programme 16.

FRIEND, Maj. Major whom Bilko tries to persuade that the men of Fort Baxter have gone made in the hope of getting a rest-cure. Is convinced when he sees Col. Hall's barnyard imitations. Ref. 'The Rest Cure' – Programme 23.

G

GAMBLERS ANONYMOUS. Organization founded by Corp. Henshaw in late rebellion against his mentor, Bilko. Ref. 'The Bilko Boycott' – Programme 141.

GANDER, Pvt. Played by Tige Andrews. Obscure member of motor pool. (See MOTOR POOL.)

GIBSON, Hoot. Cowboy hero of Montana Morgan (qv). Ref. 'Bilko's TV Pilot' – Programme 100.

GLADYS. Potential girlfriend of Bilko; his attempts to generate the money needed to take her out on a date lead to trouble. Ref. 'Bilko Talks in His Sleep' – Programme 82.

GLOW, Gloria. Hollywood actress, famed for co-starring in war movies with Rory Mundane (qv). Ref. 'Bilko In Hollywood' – Programme 17.

GOMEZ, Pvt. Played by Bernie Fein. (See MOTOR POOL.)

GOOMBAH, O Mighty. Ancient God invented by Bilko in order to prey on the horror comic-inspired susceptibility of Sgts. Grover and Ritzik and force them to return $7000 to the luckless Pvt. Lester Mendelsohn (qv). Turns out to be more real than Bilko may have supposed. Ref. 'Bilko's Black Magic' – Programme 58.

GRAZIANO, President. Previously unknown President of the United States of America celebrated at a special dinner by the motor pool whilst on the trail of the recipe to Casserole Boudereau (qv). The men sing that moving anthem, 'Hail to President Graziano, First In Peace And War'. Ref. 'The Mess Hall Mess' – Programme 61.

GROVE CITY. Small Californian town that is the location of Camp Fremont, home of the motor pool in their later days. Notable because the USO there stands in the one place in

California where gambling is legal. (Ref. 'Bilko's Casino' – Programme 138.) Only important building is the Grove City Hotel. Visiting superstar Monica Malamar (qv) has a low opinion of its royal suite: 'Better open a window. The last royalty to stay here must have been King Kong.' (Ref. 'Bilko's Hollywood Romance' – Programme 123.) In the following episode (Ref. 'Bilko's Grand Hotel' – Programme 124) Bilko buys the hotel off its owner, who is called Hilton, and tries to sell it to Conrad Hilton, owner of the hotel chain. His plans are foiled by the incompetence of his subordinates. Grove City's only other claim to fame is that it almost became the new home of the New York Yankees, as Bilko tells Mayor Rickles (qv) 'The Grove City Yankees! For the opening game you can throw the first orange. It'll give it that Californian touch.' Ref. 'Gold Fever' – Programme 108.

GROVER, M/Sgt. Francis. Played by Jimmy Little. In charge of communications at Fort Baxter and ally of M/Sgt. Rupert Ritzik (qv) in opposition to Sgt. Bilko. Marginally the less stupid of the pair, although equally poor at poker. Can only beat Bilko at cards when aided by an astutely placed mirror (Ref. 'New Recruits' – Programme 1). When he does manage to defeat Bilko retribution soon follows, as when Bilko persuades him to install a private phone in his room and invest in an entirely useless property (Ref. 'Empty Store' – Programme 2), or when he is forced to cover himself in chicken grease, place a necklace of chicken bones around his neck and abase himself before the whole motor pool in retribution for his taking Pvt. Mendelsohn's money. (See GOOMBAH, Oh Mighty above and MENDELSOHN, Pvt. Lester below.) Ref. 'Bilko's Black Magic' – Programme 58. For an analysis on his cultural tastes see RITZIK, M/Sgt. below.

GUNTHER, Wally. Man who marries WAC Pvt. Sally Fisher, thereby ruining Bilko's maternity insurance plan. Ref. 'Bilko's Insurance Company' –Programme 104.

H

HALL, Col. John T. 'Melonhead'. Commander of troops at Fort Baxter and Camp Fremont. Knows that he is 'an unknown colonel at a forgotten post', but dreams of becoming 'an officer of stature and military importance'. Knows that Bilko is the main obstacle preventing this from occurring, e.g. when he has a chimp inducted into the army by mistake: 'Will they remember me as a West Point officer who was cited for bravery in two wars? No, they'll remember me as the man who opened the door of the army to the animal kingdom.' (Ref. 'The Court Martial' – Programme 28.) Is constantly hoping for attention from the Pentagon, but is amazed or terrified when it arrives: 'The Pentagon? Calling this post? They must have the wrong number. Maybe we're at war – did anyone hear anything on the radio this morning?' (Ref. 'Bilko in Hollywood' – Programme 17.) We know little about his past, other than that he spent some of his WWII service in Australia and that he married Nell Hall (qv) at the age of twenty-six after a three-year courtship (Ref. 'Bilko's Allergy' – Programme 114). But there is also mysterious talk of his having served up 'strong lemonade' during his wild cadet days at West Point (Ref. 'Army Memoirs' – Programme 25). Perhaps there is more to the Col. than meets the eye. His relationship with Bilko is discussed more fully in 'Bilko and the Colonel'.

HALL, Mrs Hall. Long-suffering wife of Col. Hall. Has a soft spot for Bilko as a result of his ceaseless flattery (Ref. 'The Twitch' – Programme 12), but is also the focus of Doberman's hypnotized attention (Ref. 'The Big Scandal' – Programme 65).

HENSHAW, Cpl. Played by Alan Melvyn. Is, along with Cpl. Rocco Barbella, Bilko's loyal sidekick, although he exhibits from the first a somewhat more cynical attitude towards his boss than does the Italian. Towards the end this becomes progressively more pronounced, as when he remarks – seeing the sarge smell the night air for the scent of gambling – 'It's like radar. He sends out waves of greed and they bounce back when they hit money' (Ref. 'Bilko's Allergy' – Programme 114). By the penultimate episode, 'The Bilko Boycott', Henshaw has set up Gamblers Anonymous in order to combat Ernie, but this does not prevent him ending up in the guardhouse with his master at the end of the series.

HIGGENS, Pvt. Super-keen rookie who drives Bilko crazy by insisting he stick to the rule-book, 'You see, sir, I'm going to stay in the armed forces.' 'Wouldn't you be much happier in the navy,' asks Bilko. Higgins then lapses and loses all the recruits' money to Grover, Sowici and Pendleton in a game of poker, not realizing that playing the game in college is a very different proposition from taking on three hardened army sergeants. This forces Bilko into action on his side in order to recover the money. Refs. 'New Recruits' – Programme 1, and 'The Empty Store' – Programme 2.

HODGES, Ellen. Briefly girlfriend of Bilko after Joan Hogan (qv). Played by Hildy Parks. Drives Bilko so mad with love he has to go to the police for help. Ref. 'Bilko's Big Woman Hunt' – Programme 111.

HOGAN, M/Sgt. Joan. Played by Elisabeth Fraser. Beautiful blonde WAC from Sumter, South Carolina and Bilko's only true love. He loves her and can't bear to be without her, but equally can't be with her permanently. She loves him, but makes occasional bursts of independence and canoodles with others; eg. Pvt. Mulligan (Ref. 'Bilko's Engagement' – Programme 39), Sgt. Patterson (Ref. 'Dinner at Sowici's' – Programme 24) and Randy Vandermeer (qv) (Ref. 'Joan's Big Romance' – Programme 107). After her fling with the latter she disappears from the series. See 'Bilko and the Arts of Love'.

HONERGAN, Pvt. Also known as HONNERGAR, Pvt. Played by Fred Gwynne. Occasional member of the motor pool who makes three guest-star appearances as 'The Stomach', an eating champion who can only eat when unhappy (Ref. 'The Eating Contest' – Programme 4), a quiz-show champion whose stay in the Arctic, where all he had to read was a guide to birds, has turned him into an expert ornithologist (Ref. 'It's For the Birds' – Programme 36) and the brother – he claims – of a potential Miss America (Ref. 'Miss America' – Programme 26).

HONNERGAR, Mrs Peggy. Apparently beautiful sister of Pvt. Honnergar (above), but turns out to be his mother. Ref. 'Miss America' – Programme 26.

J

JENKINS, Pvt. Hillbilly private who accidentally discovers wonders of crank oil and applejack. Ref. 'Bilko's Formula 7' – Programme 129.

JOHN'S ORIGINAL WIFE. Title of soap opera broadcast on Bilko's radio station following the accidental recording of a quarrel between Col. and Mrs Hall. Ref. 'Radio B.I.L.K.O.' – Programme 62.

K

KABUCHI ISLAND. Pacific site of WWII battle, to be featured in *Love in a Foxhole*, an epic film by C. D. Chadwick (qv). Bilko, who fought there, is sent to Hollywood as the army's technical adviser, provoking the Col. into amazement – 'Bilko representing the army – *our* army?' – and then envy – 'An expenses-paid trip to Hollywood. Who says crime does not pay?' Considerable controversy exists as to whether the battle on Kabuchi was at the north or south end of the island (see 'The Bilko Interview'). Ref. 'Bilko in Hollywood' – Programme 17.

KADOWSKI, Pvt. Stash. Played by Karl Lucas. Like Dillingham, one of the few handsome motor-pool regulars. Rumoured by Bilko to be a newly arrived Polish immigrant who can barely speak English; e.g. when it looks as though he will be picked for a film part Bilko wants: 'A wonderful choice, sir. I'll start teaching him the English language immediately. You should see him at the mess hall. He's a real chatterbox: "Me soldat, me eat." We could use subtitles.' Bilko's remarks are, as far as we can tell, untrue and slanderous – when are they ever not? Ref. 'Platoon in the Movies' – Programme 35.

KAKTABOBA FATALIS. 100 per cent fatal tropical disease diagnosed in Bilko (and invented for the purpose) by the camp doctor after Bilko has feigned illness to avoid an uncomfortable bivouac. Ref. 'Bivouac' – Programme 14.

KAYOODLE, Two-card. Card game played by the motor pool into which Bilko plans to initiate Justin Pierce in the hope of winning some of the fortune which he believes (incorrectly) that Pierce possesses. Ref. 'Bilko Goes To College' – Programme 37.

KENNEDY, George. Prominent real-life Hollywood actor often featured as a 'heavy' or in war movies. Appears as an extra, playing a Military Policeman, in the final Bilko episode . . . Ref. 'Weekend Colonel' – Programme 142.

L

LANDERS, Joy. Prominent socialite in Roseville, whose country club – founded by her father – has the only fox hunt west of Wichita. Is an immense snob and laughs at the motor pool's request that she become their carnival queen, with terrible consequences for her. Ref. 'Mardi Gras' – Programme 21. (See also 'Duane Doberman – Portrait of a Legend'.)

LA TORSO, TESSIE. Dancer at Minsky's vaudeville in Roseville who pretends to be Bilko's aunt ('She's not a Bilko, she's a Torso. I've looked up to her all my life') at a party celebrating his apparently forthcoming marriage to Joan Hogan. Ref. 'Bilko's Engagement' – Programme 39.

LOCKMAN, Hugo. New recruit, whom Bilko discovers has a brilliant playwrighting talent. Ref. 'Sgt. Bilko Presents' – Programme 80.

LONESOME SAM'S HORSE PARLOR. Betting joint in Topeka to which Bilko goes to place a bet on a 40–1 certainty, the joint is immediately raided by the police. Ref. 'Recruiting Sergeant' – Programme 33.

LUKENS, Major. Visits Fort Baxter, only to be involved in a Bilko plot to be given a furlough in order to visit a nightclub singer in Washington DC, in the course of which he is made to 'see' spaceships and an alien (actually Doberman in costume, with green skin and an illuminated hat). Ref. 'Bilko and the Flying Saucers' – Programme 83.

LUMPKIN, Pvt. Harry. Played by Dick Van Dyke. Hillbilly recruit who turns out to have a natural genius for baseball and is almost traded by Bilko to the New York Yankees. Ref. 'Hillbilly Whiz' – Programme 79.

M

McCLUSTY, Pvt. Mike. Handsome recruit with tremendous power over women, whom Bilko wants to promote as a movie star via an army poster. Ref. 'The Face on the Recruiting Poster' – Programme 40.

McMILLEN, Ed. Tough gangster and gambling boss who insults Bilko and is made by pay for his mistake to such effect that he eventually gives up the life of crime and sets up in the launderette business with his brother-in-law. Ref. 'Bilko Goes To College' – Programme 37.

MACOOCHI. An island near China to which Bilko and his men are posted, greatly against their will. Ref. 'Bilko's Chinese Restaurant' – Programme 99.

MALAMAR, Monica. Beautiful Hollywood actress with an undeniable talent for bad publicity. As Louella Parsons, Hollywood's most famous gossip, tells her; 'Monica, take my advice; if you keep fighting in nightclubs, knocking out policemen and getting married all the time, sooner or later it's going to hurt you at the box-office.' To clean up her image she is sent to Camp Fremont to be photographed with Sgt. Bilko, with whom she is to have a staged romance – the glamorous movie star and the wholesome soldier. She takes it badly at first but when she observes Bilko's talent for profitable business deals her opinion of him changes. Ref. 'Bilko's Hollywood Romance' – Programme 123.

MENDELSOHN, Pvt. Lester. Soldier marooned on desert island who picks up over $7000 in back pay. Bilko pretends that he has mastered arts of black magic, only to discover that this is, in fact, the truth. Ref. 'Bilko's Black Magic' – Programme 58.

MERRIWETHER, Lee. Real-life Miss America of 1955 who appears in the Bilko episode of the same title. Ref. 'Miss America' – Programme 91.

MIDDLETON, Lillian. The daughter of a Roseville millionaire, buxom and not too attractive, who falls in love with Doberman, much against her parents' wishes. Ref. 'His Highness, Doberman' – Programme 71.

MIGNON. Beautiful French girl, who calls Bilko 'Papa', much to his embarrassment. Ref. 'Papa Bilko' – Programme 77.

MORGAN, Bonnie. Singer at the Dee Cee Club in Washington, with whom Bilko has a date, which results in him faking the arrival of UFOs (See LUKENS, Maj. above). Ref. 'Bilko and the Flying Saucers' – Programme 83.

MORGAN, Pvt. Montana. Rootin'-tootin' cowboy and Buffalo Soup lover who arrives in motor pool, where his exuberance drives the others crazy. Fender, 'Look, one shoulder is lower than the other from those clouts on the back', Zimmerman, 'He keeps picking me up. I got eight hours flying time.' Bilko sells him to Ritzik for $75, but then has to get him back fast when it looks as though he may have a bright future as a TV cowboy. Ref. 'Bilko's TV Pilot' – Programme 100.

MOTOR POOL. Bilko's men, whom he simultaneously rips off whenever possible and defends to the last. His feelings for them can best be gauged by his remarks in 'The Bilko Interview' above. As for their actual work, we only occasionally see them doing any, which might explain why Col. Hall has to wait so long to have his jeep or staff car repaired. Their mechanical techniques are, at best, eccentric; Bilko hates them to do things by the army manual and when they do he becomes furious – 'I spend years trying to teach these guys to become mechanics and what do I get? Bookworms. Show me in the army manual where it says you can mend a carburettor with Juicy Fruit.' Ref. 'Platoon in the Movies' – Programme 35. The full staff of the motor pool includes Cpls. Barbella and Henshaw and Pvts. Dillingham, Doberman, Fender, Fleischman, Gander, Gomez, Kadowski, Mullen, Palmer, Paparelli and Sugarman.

MULLEN, Pvt. Played by Jack Healey. Member of motor pool (see above).

MUNDANE, Rory. Star of C. D. Chadwick's (qv) blockbuster war films. Credits include *They Met on Okinawa* and *Iwo Jima Baby*, both of which co-starred the delectable Gloria Glow (qv). Set to play Sgt. Skinner in battle epic *Guns, Guts and Gals* set on Kabuchi Island (qv). Film is tribute to American GIs: 'They made the Japs say "Uncle" and the girls say, "More, more, more." Their battle flag was a torn sarong, but they blasted their way to Tokyo.' Bilko called in as military adviser to film, whose title has now been changed to *Love In a Foxhole* ('Gals is crude' – C. D. Chadwick). Bilko claims Skinner was actually a squint-eyed midget who lisped. Re-casts Mundane as himself following inability of studio to find anyone else young, handsome and virile enough to play the part. Film abandoned. Ref. 'Bilko in Hollywood' – Programme 17.

N

NAGY, Pvt. Steve. Hungarian member of the motor pool who continually heads back home to his family and after whom Bilko has to chase. Ref. 'A.W.O.L.' – Programme 8.

NEWMAN, Blinkie. Roseville bookie and local operator for Ed McMillen (qv). Educates his boss, who thinks Bilko is just another dumb soldier: 'I'm no sucker. I wouldn't touch Bilko with a ten-foot pole. I closed the books on him years ago.' Ref. 'Bilko Goes To College' – Programme 37.

O

OPERATION MOONBEAM. Attempt to flush out gambling

from Fort Baxter, organized by Col. Hall. Ref. 'The Colonel's Reunion' – Programme 92.

OWITASHI, Treaty of. Treaty signed by Cherokee Indians giving Oklahoma to the Americans. Bilko, as Chief Bald Eagle (qv) claims that it is invalid and almost forces US to buy the state back for $50,000,000 before it is revealed that the treaty might be genuine after all. Ref. 'Cherokee Ernie' – Programme 81.

P

PALMER, Pvt. Played by Jay Sidney. Undistinguished motor pool regular (see MOTOR POOL).

PAPARELLI, Pvt. Dino. Played by Billy Sands. After Duane Doberman the most prominent member of the motor pool. Chirpy, but able to put on great melodramatic acts; for example, when conning Col. Hall out of $300 tax rebate on pretence that he needs it to get married when it will actually go towards Bilko's poker bankroll (Ref. 'Bilko's Allergy' – Programme 114). Also, like Doberman, has whole episodes built around him, e.g. 'Warrant Officer Paparelli' – Programme 130, in which Bilko has him 'save' a general's life three times in order to get him promoted to officer rank, with unfortunate results, or 'Bilko's Honeymoon' – Programme 98, in which Dino has to go to Florida as Bilko's 'wife'. Also joins navy accidentally in search of a monster crap game (Ref. 'Bilko Joins the Navy' – Programme 115). Is more or less the least incompetent of Bilko's men and therefore the one most often trusted with the important chores that form the mechanics of a typical Bilko plot. Is not, however, totally reliable; e.g. when he helps burn down the hotel Bilko is about to sell to Conrad Hilton (Ref. 'Bilko's Grand Hotel' – Programme 124).

PAPOWKSI, Hilda. Roseville barmaid and girlfriend of J. J. Coogan, the Fort Baxter quartermaster. Is put into Bilko's TV Western in order to persuade Coogan to hand over some film equipment and then actually becomes a star in TV series 'Frontier Gal'. Ref. 'Bilko's TV Pilot' – Programme 100.

PARADISE BAR AND GRILL. Louche Roseville hostelry, otherwise known as The Snakepit, run by the formidable Mildred and regularly patronized by the motor pool.

PARKER, Lt. Special Services officer assigned to Fort Baxter in an attempt to raise morale and cut out gambling on the post – an impossible task. Ref. 'The Centennial' – Programme 13.

PARKER, Pvt. An insubordinate petty hoodlum assigned to the motor pool who jeopardizes Bilko's chances of a five-day pass until the Sgt. ropes him into a scheme to rob Ft. Knox. Ref. 'The Hoodlum' – Programme 7.

PELVIN, Elvin. Also known as Elvin Pilbeam, Irving Melvin, Edwin, Elmer, etc. Famed rock'n'roll superstar. Drafted by the army, but immediately the cause of mass hysteria. Moved from Ft. Dix to Ft. Henry, from the Deep South to the West Coast, but followed everywhere by fans. Taken to Washington; moved from hotel to Pentagon successfully, 'But we lost a tank.' General orders Pelvin to 'the smallest, most isolated, most unimportant outpost in the US army'. Fort Baxter chosen and Pelvin assigned to motor pool. Bilko's reaction: 'On golden wings a million dollars have flown into our laps. We won't be greedy – only a steady $10,000 a week.' Enlists Pelvin in motor pool's glee club, gets him special sequinned uniform. Inspired by Pelvin's latest hit 'You Ain't Nothin' but a Racoon', Bilko writes 'Brown Suede Combat Boots' (qv). Problem: Pelvin only sings when unhappy. Bilko tries to make him homesick by holding a Southern evening. But Pelvin still too happy. 'The happier he is, the poorer we get,' says Bilko. Elvin set to work with Doberman. Sings because Duane's eyes remind him of his hound dog. Attempts at recording him fail because Doberman sings along. Elvin says: 'All my life people have been trying to take advantage of me. This is the first time I've felt like I'm around friends. Sgt. Bilko just accepted me and I've written a song about it I'd like you to hear.' Sings 'Bilko is the Best' to tune of 'Love Me Tender' by little-known contemporary singer Elvis Presley. Bilko deeply moved. 'You guys have this song in your heart, who needs the record.' Smashes his recording. Ref. 'Rock'n'Roll Rookie' – Programme 57.

PENFIELD III, Herbert. Bilko lookalike who is a New York multi-millionaire. Bilko is mistaken for him while on furlough and finds himself, with Barbella and Henshaw (qv) leading a luxurious life. Penfield, visiting relatives near Fort Baxter, finds quite the opposite. Ref. 'Bilko's Double Life' – Programme 76.

PERKINS, Pvt. Supposedly orphaned draftee. Sent to motor pool after being thrown out of fourteen other army camps. Inveterate practical joker who tries Bilko's patience to its limits. Ref. 'The Son of Bilko' – Programme 56.

PETROFF, Emile. Famous Hollywood director in classic style –

beret, riding crop, excruciating accent. Tests out Bilko for lead role in *The Three Musketeers* as a ploy to separate him from Monica Malamar (qv). Ref. 'Bilko's Hollywood Romance' – Programme 123.

PETTIGUILD, Congressman. One of three sent to Fort Baxter to investigate military waste (see COLBY, Congressman). Ref. 'The Big Investigation' – Programme 16.

PORTER, Polly. WAC at Fort Baxter who turns out to be a sharpshooter. Bilko tries to promote her as a new Annie Oakley. Ref. 'Bilko's Sharpshooter' – Programme 128.

R

RIPLEY, Cpl. Blanche. WAC secretary. When the colonel's secretary leaves, Bilko decides to make sure her replacement is friendly to him. Cpl. Ripley however is angry at having to leave her soldier boyfriend and makes Bilko's platoon take all the unpleasant jobs. Ref. 'Bilko and the Colonel's Secretary' – Programme 88.

RITZIK, Sgt. Rupert. M/Sgt. and Co. Cook. Played by Joe E. Ross. Replaced Sergeant Stanley Sowici (qv) in the mess hall after the first season. Instinct plays a large part in his culinary achievements: 'I knew that chicken fricasee was good from the way it stuck to my hand.' He revealed his talents as a communicator with his programme 'Kitchen Magic Time' on 'Radio Station B.I.L.K.O.' – Programme 63.

Most of us, however, remember this 'Lucretia Borgia of Fort Baxter' with his ally, Sergeant Grover (qv) as the worst poker players on the base, always taken for their pay by Bilko. Francis and Rupert share the same endearing attachment to TV westerns, comic books, horror films and the humour of Buddy Bickford (qv). As Count Ritzik of Transylvania he nearly breaks into Hollywood pictures after Bilko convinces him he is turning into a vampire. Ref. 'Bilko's Vampire' – Programme 112. The only bet he has ever won with Bilko is one that his name wasn't Ritzik – a sucker bet Bilko made to prove that he wasn't out to fleece Ritzik of his leaving gratuity – Ref. 'A Mess Sergeant Can't Win' – Programme 43. When Ritzik spends his fifteenth wedding anniversary playing poker with Bilko, the long suffering Emma Ritzik leaves him. She returns after strenuous efforts by Bilko – Programme 93.

ROCKFORD, Lord and Lady. A millionaire couple who identify Doberman as their long-lost son. Ref. 'Doberman, Missing Heir' – Programme 137.

ROGERS, Mr and Mrs Jason. Rich couple who live on Nob Hill. Bilko wangles an invitation to their mansion through the USO, hoping to meet a rich heiress. Ref. 'Bilko the Butler' – Programme 134.

ROSA. A young Italian girl. She was engaged to Rocco Barbella's brother, Angie, when young. When she arrives in New York, he thinks her not sophisticated enough, so Bilko helps out with the 'My Fair Lady' treatment. Ref. 'The Girl From Italy' – Programme 41.

ROXBURY, Lieut. WAC Special Services officer. This beautiful blonde and her equally beautiful red-headed assistant, Cpl. Sandburg, cause havoc for Bilko when their attractions draw the men away from gambling and into the lecture halls. Ref. 'Bilko's War Against Culture' – Programme 38.

S

SANDBURG, Cpl. WAC Special Services member. Assistant to Lieut. Roxbury (qv).

SANDERS, Skinny. Talented bop drummer. When he joins the motor pool, Bilko decides to form a band to tour Europe for the army. Ref. 'Bilko's Bopster' – Programme 122.

SCHMILL UNIVERSITY. Est. 1841. Noted more for its cultivation of things of the mind, Schmill has a football team which opens the season against Notre Dame and has never lost by less than 100 to nil. Bilko arrives to teach motor pool techniques to the students, sees the weedy team and asks if Blue Cross medical insurance arranged the game. They go off to shower and Bilko recommends the buddy system in case one of them goes down the drain. When Bilko becomes coach however, speculation becomes rife that Schmill will beat Notre Dame for the first time. Ref. 'Bilko Goes to College' – Programme 37.

SNEAD, Sam. Celebrated professional golf player ('The Sweet Swing'). Plays himself in an episode where Bilko wants the colonel off the camp and enlists Snead's help to persuade him to enter the officers' golf tournament in Palm Springs, California. Ref. 'The Colonel Breaks Par' – Programme 69.

SOWICI, M/Sgt. Stanley. As he describes it: 'I am mess sergeant of Company B. Responsible for the nutritive welfare and health of over 1400 men of Fort Baxter.' This means he is Company Cook. After the first season he is replaced by Ritzik (qv) in the mess hall. Played by Harry Clark. Sowici is married in domestic blitz to Agnes (Ref. 'Dinner at Sowicis' – Programme 24).

SPEAKUP, Pvt. Harry. Name taken by Zippo the Chimp on his induction into the US Army. This remarkable proof of the army's democratic nature occurred at Fort Baxter during an exercise to induct 309 men in less than two hours, using Captain Barker's system. One of the draftees has vaudeville act, 'Charlie and Chico' with Zippo; his brother was meant to collect him at the station but didn't turn up. Through a remarkable series of oversights, the chimp passes through feet inspection, dental inspection, intelligence test and psychiatric investigation, the mistake being discovered just as the men are being sworn in. The colonel sees his chance for a brilliant coup of army efficiency turned to disgrace. In conditions of near-hysteria the camp is sealed off and a court martial convened – the chimp has bitten Sowici (qv) in the mess hall. With Bilko for defence, however, Zippo is acquitted. Finally Zippo is released from the army on compassionate grounds as the sole support of his owner and his family. An episode of consummate brilliance. Ref. 'The Court Martial' – Programme 28.

SPENCER, Captain. Naval officer in command of an aircraft carrier out of San Diego. Accidentally shanghais Bilko, Paparelli and Zimmerman as they try to break into a huge navy crap game. As they steam towards a six-month tour in Alaskan waters, Bilko tries to convince the crew that Spencer is going barmy. Ref. 'Bilko Joins the Navy' – Programme 115.

SPINOZA, Barry. Psychiatrist and noted opponent of Sigmund Freud known only to Bilko who explains his views at great length in 'Bilko Gets Some Sleep' – Programme 49.

STANFORD UNIVERSITY. Celebrated North American University. Proud of being asked to be a godfather, Bilko tries to wangle the child a place in the class of 1977. Ref. 'Bilko's Godson' – Programme 132.

SULLIVAN, Ed. Famous American chat-show host. He plays himself in two Bilko shows: 'Sergeant Bilko Presents Ed Sullivan' – Programme 48 where Bilko takes over an army special planned for the Ed Sullivan show with his big production number of 'Granada'; and 'Show Segments' – Programme 70 in which the

Bilko cast and Sullivan sit down in Lindy's restaurant in New York and watch sequences cut from past episodes because of length.

T

TEXAS, Temple. Beautiful blonde planted in Ritzik's house to make Emma Ritzik jealous after she walks out on him. Ref. 'Bilko Saves Ritzik's Marriage' – Programme 93.

THOMPSON, Carlisle. Ex-GI friend of Bilko's and son of a millionaire shipper in New York. His great love is sculpture, but his father wants him to go into the business. Bilko on furlough prefers the luxury of the Thompson mansion, but is forced to follow Carlisle into a Greenwich Village garret after a family quarrel. Bilko admires Carlisle's work, *Woman With Grapes*: 'If you put a clock in it, it'll give it novelty value.' Ref. 'Bilko, the Art Lover' – Programme 94.

THOMPSON, Pvt. Member of the motor pool platoon, sole heir to $200 million automobile fortune. Bilko tries to get Thompson to bankroll him to buy the Paradise Bar and Grill. Ref. 'Rich Kid' – Programme 15.

THOMPSON, Red. GI, whose life Bilko saved on Saipan during WWII. Claims to have a diamond mine which he wishes to share with his rescuer. Ref. 'The Big Man Hunt' – Programme 72.

TODD, Mike. Director of the film of *Around the World in Eighty Days*. Plays himself in a spoof of the film. Ref. 'Bilko Goes Round the World' – Programme 60.

TONY. Bilko's barber. For seven years Tony has used Bilko as a testing ground for various hair restoring experiments. The quest takes on new urgency when Joan Hogan dumps Bilko for a corporal with a fine head of hair. Ref. 'Hair' – Programme 18.

TWIN OAK FLATS. A derelict property which Bilko turns into a nightclub. Ref. 'Bilko Buys a Club' – Programme 78.

TWINHAZY, Morgan. Friend of Bilko's from the army, now on Wall Street. Bilko takes his career in hand and he makes a meteoric climb to success. Ref. 'Bilko on Wall Street' – Programme 34.

'THE TWITCH'. Nickname given to Mrs Whitney (qv) for her interesting nervous habit. Ref. 'The Twitch' – Programme 12.

V

VANDERMEER, Randy. Wealthy Chicago playboy. Joan Hogan gets caught with him on a train and is photographed in a national magazine. Bilko becomes extremely jealous. Ref. 'Joan's Big Romance' – Programme 107.

W

WALLACE, Lieut. New Company Commander for Bilko's motor pool. His 'eager beaver' hard-working style makes Bilko decide that marriage is the only thing that will soften him and make him ease up on the platoon. He chooses a new WAC officer, Lieut. Rogers, as his future bride and tries to throw them together as much as possible. Unfortunately they are already engaged and trying to keep it secret. Ref. 'Bilko, The Marriage Broker' – Programme 64.

W.B.B.H. Call sign of a radio station set up by Bilko when the Roseville local station closes down. He uses army equipment to broadcast and draws on the Fort Baxter personnel to fill up air time: Doberman giving news analysis, Ritzik with mess hall recipes and, unknown to them, the colonel and Nell Hall recorded and broadcast as a soap opera. Ref. 'Radio Station B.I.L.K.O.' – Programme 63.

WHAT EVERY YOUNG SPARK PLUG SHOULD KNOW. Title of unusual training film made by the motor pool platoon. Bilko says: 'Training films are the army's answer to sleeping pills' and shows them how, with a Busby Berkeley extravaganza on the maintenance of the spark plug. Doberman plays an innocent young spark plug who escapes from the fatal attractive charms of Sludge (played by Virginia DeLuce). Bilko warns him away, showing what happened to him, a broken-down old spark plug. His number 'There's still a spark left in the old plug tonight' ends the film complete with a chorus of WAC dancing girls. The film wows the Pentagon after a general discovers it has taught his wife the basics of car maintenance.

WHITEAGLE, Cpl. Charlie. Red Indian army chum of Bilko's. When Bilko stays with his parents he becomes involved in a land dispute, is made a member of Cherokee tribe and discovers Oklahoma still belongs to the Indians. Ref. 'Cherokee Ernie' – Programme 81.

WHITNEY, Capt. and Mrs. Special Services Officer and his wife, who come to Fort Baxter to help solve the gambling problem. Mrs Whitney intends delivering her celebrated lecture on 'The Life and Works of Ludwig van Beethoven' and Bilko is given the task of filling the lecture hall. He has no takers until it is revealed that Mrs Whitney is 'The Twitch', when commercial possibilities cause a stampede for tickets. Ref. 'The Twitch' – Programme 12.

WINGATE, Mr. Philadelphian millionaire. His daughter plans to marry the son of a Fort Baxter sergeant, but Wingate refuses to invite a mere sergeant to the wedding. Bilko storms off on his behalf. Ref. 'The Blue Blood of Bilko' – Programme 51.

Y

YWCA, in New York. Bilko and Joan Hogan on furlough both stay here separately, sharing a steam bath and dormitory without recognizing each other. Ref. 'Furlough' – Programme 27.

Z

ZABODA, Madame. Medium and adviser to Ritzik, Camp Fremont's most gullible sergeant. Her plan to steal Ritzik's raffle winnings is foiled by Bilko. Ref. 'Bilko and the Medium' – Programme 121.

ZIMMERMAN, Pvt. Fielding. Played by Mickey Freeman. Member of the motor pool platoon. Immortalized in a line from 'Rock'n'Roll Rookie' – Programme 57; Elvin Pelvin, homesick for the Deep South, asks, 'Hey, are you boys Southern?' Bilko replies: 'Southern? Here Zimmerman, give him some grits.'

The Complete Bilkography

The digits following '35' in the serial numbers quoted below are the numbers of the episodes as used throughout the book. The list below is in order of transmission, which did not necessarily follow the numerical sequence.

The names of writers are given wherever known.

First Series
Produced and staged by Nat Hiken

Directed by Al De Caprio
Photographed by William J. Miller
Supervised by Edward J. Montagne
Editors: Sy Singer, Ray Sandiford
Art Directors: Don Gilman, Al Brenner
Production Manager: M. Clay Adams
Music: John Strauss
Additional Music: Hank Sylvern
Recording Engineer: James Shields
Assistant to Producer: Kevin Pines
Settings: Jack Landau
Filmed by Kenco Films Inc.

Audition Show   26 August 1955
The pilot show of the series introducingBilko and the members of the camp.

New Recruits   20 September 1955 3501
Written by Nat Hiken
Fellow sergeants Sowici, Grover and Pendleton clean Bilko

out of $250. He tries to raise a bankroll for Saturday's game, but the PX rapidly sells out of money belts when the news spreads. Then Bilko is given a squad of new recruits to train ...

Empty Store 27 September 1955 3502
Written by Nat Hiken

Bilko is frozen out of further poker games on camp when he is broke and swears revenge. He rents an empty store in the nearby town of Roseville, but refuses to say why. The boys at Fort Baxter try desperately for a piece of the action which they're sure Bilko is cooking, but he refuses their dollars even when offered on bended knees. Then the speculation starts a real property boom ...

WAC (A.k.a. 'Personal Transportation Provided') 4 October 1955 3510
Written by Nat Hiken and Arnold Auerbach

Fort Baxter needs a volunteer sergeant to check the armoury once a day – and the job carries a personal jeep with it. By careful scheming Bilko manages to dissuade other sergeants from going for the post – but a new sergeant at the camp applies. Bilko has to compete with a woman, who is beautiful and a disciple of his own methods. (First appearance of Elisabeth Fraser as Bilko's sweetheart, WAC Sergeant Joan Hogan.)

The Horse 11 October 1955 3503
Written by Nat Hiken, Terry Ryan and Barry Blitzer

At a country fair Bilko and the platoon buy an ailing racehorse, 'Bellboy', which they hope to cure and train as a winner. Feed presents no problem after Bilko persuades the camp dietician to test oats on his men for their nutritive value, nor does accommodation in the camp's unused guest house, at least until a visiting general decides to stay ... (First appearance of Hope Sansberry as Colonel Hall's wife.)

A.W.O.L. 18 October 1955 3508
Written by Nat Hiken

Private Steve Nagy always heads for home, with or without permission, when there is trouble in his Hungarian family. Bilko is sent off to fetch him back from Chicago and runs straight into a family feud over the marriage plans of Nagy's sister. Bilko tries to sort things out, makes them even worse, but finally reconciles the families – not before almost finding himself AWOL.

Boxer   25 October 1955 3520
Written by Nat Hiken, Terry Ryan and Barry Blitzer

When Bilko learns that Private Claude Dillingham of his platoon is a former Golden Gloves champion, he puts his money on him in the camp boxing tournament. Then he learns that Dillingham's girlfriend, Felicia, won't let him fight any more. Bilko gets a sailor to insult Felicia in Dillingham's presence, but she proves perfectly capable of looking after herself. Dillingham prefers cultivating chrysanthemums to fighting, so Bilko then encourages a hatred of flowers in his opponent. (First appearance of Terry Carter as 'Sugie' Sugarman).

The Hoodlum   1 November 1955 3507
Written by Nat Hiken

Bilko smartens up his platoon in order to win the 'Soldier of the Month' award with its prize of a five-day pass. Unfortunately an insubordinate recruit assigned to him, Private Parker, has only one intention – to get out of the army, through a dishonourable discharge if necessary. Bilko's plan to win the award and whittle the petty hoodlum down to size includes involving him in a plan to rob Fort Knox . . .

Mardi Gras   (A.k.a. 'The Motor Pool Mardi Gras') 8 November 1955 3521
Written by Nat Hiken, Terry Ryan and Barry Blitzer

The Fort Baxter Motor Pool Mardi Gras invites a local socialite, Joy Landers, to reign as queen of their festivities – with Private Doberman as her king. When she refuses, Bilko decides to teach her a lesson and soon the rumour is spreading around town about 'that different kind of international playboy, Duane Doberman'. Joy's curiosity is at fever pitch; but when Bilko reveals the truth about Doberman her reaction surprises everyone.

Eating Contest   15 November 1955 3504
Written by Nat Hiken and Arnold Auerbach

In a forthcoming camp eating contest, Bilko is quick to put his money on a private in his platoon, Honnergan, known as 'The Stomach' through his previous championship-winning prowess. Bilko soon realizes, however, that Honnergan can only eat when he is miserable and reminded of his broken romances, so Bilko sets out to make him the unhappiest GI in the army.

The Centennial (A.k.a. '100th Anniversary') 22 November 1955 3513

Written by Nat Hiken, Terry Ryan and Barry Blitzer

When Colonel Hall orders him to stop all gambling among the enlisted men on the post, the new eager beaver Lieutenant Parker from Special Services starts classes in painting, dancing and other arts. Bilko fights back by staging a pageant for the camp's 100th anniversary in honour of its past heroes, a show which does not, however, present either the camp or Lieutenant Parker in a good light.

Bivouac (A.k.a. 'Sick Call Ernie') 29 November 1955 3514

Written by Nat Hiken, Terry Ryan and Barry Blitzer

When manoeuvres start for the camp Bilko is usually found on sick call with some rare disease. This time it's 'kaktaboba fatalis' dreamed up by the camp doctor and invariably fatal. But Colonel Hall is determined to deal severely with his 'ailing' sergeant and soon Bilko is wishing he was out of hospital and out marching with a full pack through the rain.

Singing Contest (A.k.a. 'Singing Platoon') 6 December 1955 3509

Written by Nat Hiken, Terry Ryan and Barry Blitzer

It is 14° below zero at Fort Baxter when Bilko hears of the singing contest organized by Special Services. The first prize is a free trip to Miami, so the platoon start practising immediately. Unfortunately they are so bad that Bilko secretly decides to bet the entire platoon welfare fund that they will lose. When they improve dramatically on discovering an excellent tenor in Private Brubaker (who tends the furnace) Bilko is in a quandary.

The Twitch (A.k.a. 'The Lecture') 13 December 1955 3512

Written by Nat Hiken, Terry Ryan and Barry Blitzer

Colonel Hall orders Bilko to provide an audience for a lecture on Beethoven as a punishment for his gambling. He has no takers until he learns that the officer's wife giving the talk is known as 'The Twitch' after her nervous habit.

Bilko has only to open a book on the number of twitches for the tickets to sell like hot cakes.

Reunion   20 December 1955 3506
Written by Nat Hiken and Arnold Auerbach

Bilko is impressed at a reunion in New York by the success of his wartime comrades in business. He feels sorry for himself and jumps at the chance of a job which one of the executives offers him. A short sample of New York business life convinces Bilko that the army isn't so bad after all.

Rich Kid   (A.k.a. 'The Platoon's Saloon') 27 December 1955 3515
Written by Nat Hiken

Stumped for funds to buy the Paradise Bar and Grill in Roseville, Bilko thinks he's hit the jackpot when he discovers one of his platoon, Private Thompson, is the sole heir to a $200 million automobile fortune. He pretends that he knows nothing about Thompson but gets the platoon to make his bed, do his work and lend him money. Bilko thinks it's like taking candy from a baby; he takes Thompson to the saloon, buys him a few beers and introduces him to one of the girls, but discovers the rich recruit has more business sense than Bilko credited.

Hollywood   3 January 1956 3517
Written by Nat Hiken

Cecil D. Chadwick Productions of Hollywood plan a new war picture based on the battle in the Pacific for Kabuchi Island. The Pentagon has grave misgivings but sends a soldier – Bilko – who was at the battle to act as 'technical adviser'. Bilko causes havoc at the studio, finding fault with the production and insisting it is rewritten to include his famous charge. Eventually the studio cancels the film in despair and a grateful Pentagon awards Bilko a thirty-day furlough. (Guest appearance of songwriter Jule Styne as himself.)

Investigation   (A.k.a. 'The Big Investigation') 10 January 1956 3516
Written by Nat Hiken, Terry Ryan and Barry Blitzer

A Congressional Committee arrives at Fort Baxter to investigate military waste. Bilko persuades Colonel Hall to let him show the Congressmen around – they discover his platoon barefoot, receiving food parcels from Europe and playing baseball without bats or balls. His aim is to win a $10 a month raise for all GIs, but eventually finds the quickest way is to challenge the three committee members to poker.

Kids in Trailer (A.k.a. 'Operation Diapers') 17 January 1956 3505

Written by Nat Hiken, Terry Ryan and Barry Blitzer

Bilko does a good turn for a member of his platoon by baby-sitting in a trailer so the GI can take a three-day furlough with his wife. He panics when he finds himself unable to change the baby's nappy, and calls the wife of a Fort Baxter sergeant who has six children. The sergeant has been transferred and Bilko uses the military radio network to contact him through several army camps and across the Atlantic to Germany.

Revolutionary War (A.k.a. 'Revolution') 24 January 1956 3519

Written by Nat Hiken, Terry Ryan and Barry Blitzer

Bilko's Aunt Minerva sends him a diary showing that his great, great uncle, Major Joshua Bilko, was on George Washington's staff during the American Revolution. Flushed with pride, Bilko determines to reform and apply for Officer Training School. The platoon is amazed at the transformation until Bilko reads the diary aloud to them and it becomes clear that Bilko's great, great uncle had much in common with his descendant.

Transfer 31 January 1956 3522

Written by Nat Hiken, Vincent Bogert and Harvey Orkin

When Colonel Hall reprimands Bilko for using his staff car on dates, Bilko puts in for a transfer and gets it. The men at the new post, however, are so gullible that Bilko soon gets bored taking their money and back at Fort Baxter his replacement turns out to be a rule-book martinet who keeps the whole post on its toes. Colonel Hall is thwarted in his search for the quiet life and yearns for Bilko's return.

The Rest Cure 7 February 1956 3523

Written by Nat Hiken, Vincent Bogert and Harvey Orkin

The camp is suffering a heatwave and Bilko tries to raise money for a vacation by staging a talent contest in which

Colonel Hall does impersonations of farm animals. It fails, but Bilko then hears of an army rest centre in the cool Rockies and gets his men to act crazy. A Pentagon major is sent to check out the post and finds Fort Baxter is like a loony bin, commanded by an officer who makes barnyard noises.

Dinner at Sowici's   14 February 1956 3524

Written by Nat Hiken, Harvey Orkin and Barry Blitzer

Bilko gets worried that Sergeant Joan Hogan is trying to trap him into marriage and determines to drive all such thoughts out of her head. But she turns all his arguments back on him and when he tries to finish the romance, she makes him jealous by ignoring him for the favours of a handsome sergeant. Finally he gets the pair of them invited to dinner at the home of the Sowicis, hoping that a sight of their domestic battlefield will put her off marriage.

Army Memoirs   21 February 1956 3525

Written by Nat Hiken, Harvey Orkin and Barry Blitzer

Sergeants Pendleton, Grover and Sowici refuse to be fall guys for Bilko any longer and get him busted to private by telling Colonel Hall of his misdeeds. He warns them that within six hours they'll be begging the colonel to give him back his stripes and tells everyone that he is writing his army memoirs. He intends revealing his comrades' scandalous pasts – Colonel Hall's included, particularly the story about some 'strong lemonade' he served at West Point.

Miss America   28 February 1956 3526

Written by Nat Hiken, Arnie Rosen, Coleman Jacoby, Terry Ryan and Barry Blitzer

The platoon are kidding Private Honnegar for not having a girl, but change their tune when he shows them a picture of a beautiful girl and tells them it's his hometown sweetheart, Peggy. Bilko enters her in a beauty contest as the army's 'mystery girl' and on the telephone persuades her to enter what she thinks is a baking contest. She turns up just before the contest and Bilko discovers she is Honnegar's mother aged sixty and the picture was taken years before.

The Court-Martial   (A.k.a. 'The Case of Harry Speak-up') 6 March 1956 3528

Written by Nat Hiken, Coleman Jacoby and Arnie Rosen

During an attempt to speed up the procedures for inducting soldiers into the army, Zippo the Chimpanzee, who belongs to one of the inductees, is accidentally enrolled in the United States Army. Realizing with horror what they've done, Colonel Hall and a visiting general decide the only way out is to court-martial Zippo and they appoint Bilko as his defence.

Furlough in New York   13 March 1956 3527
Written by Nat Hiken and Terry Ryan

Both Bilko and Sergeant Joan Hogan apply for furloughs in New York, but don't tell each other their destinations since they think the other wants to have some fun on his own. However, in the city Bilko finds all his old girlfriends married, and Joan can't line up a blind date. When he mistakes the YWCA for the YMCA, Bilko shares a steam bath and a dormitory with Joan without either of them recognizing the other. When they get back to camp they have difficulty explaining how they managed accidentally to exchange dog tags.

The Big Uranium Strike   20 March 1956 3529
Written by Nat Hiken, Tony Webster, Coleman Jacoby and Arnie Rosen

Bilko suspects there are uranium deposits under Fort Baxter and sends Doberman out one night with a Geiger counter. When Colonel Hall demands to know what is going on, Bilko and Doberman find a strong signal in the colonel's living room. Bilko persuades the colonel that his house is infested with termites and when he leaves the platoon Bilko starts digging. But the colonel returns just as Bilko is dynamiting the cellar.

Bilko and the Beast   27 March 1956 3531
Written by Nat Hiken, Tony Webster, Coleman Jacoby and Arnie Rosen

Colonel Hall sends for a hard-boiled sergeant, Quentin B. Benson, usually known as 'The Beast', to make soldiers out of Bilko and his platoon. Unable to get the better of The Beast physically or at poker, Bilko tries psychological warfare and takes out a $100,000 life insurance policy on the sergeant's life with himself, Rocco and Henshaw as beneficiaries.

The Physical Check-up (A.k.a. 'Physical') 10 April 1956 3532

Written by Nat Hiken, Coleman Jacoby and Arnie Rosen

Colonel Hall excuses Bilko from leading his men on a 20-mile hike and announces physical exams for all sergeants. Bilko suspects the army of trying to get him a medical discharge and begins an exhausting routine of exercise. When he's examined the medical officer declares him the first case of combat fatigue in peacetime.

Recruiting Sergeant 17 April 1956 3523

Written by Nat Hiken, Tony Webster and Terry Ryan

All men at Fort Baxter are restricted to the base by the colonel, who is off to Topeka on a recruitment drive. Bilko gets a hot 40–1 race tip from a GI friend whose life he saved on Okinawa. In order to get off the base and bet the platoon's welfare fund, Bilko persuades the colonel to take him with him. Looking for Lonesome Sam's Horse Parlor Bilko gets saddled with five recruits who are ordered not to leave his side. They find the parlor just before it's raided by the Topeka police.

Hair (A.k.a. 'The Barber Shop') 24 April 1956 3518

Written by Nat Hiken, Terry Ryan, Barry Blitzer and Arnold Auerbach

Previously impervious to jokes about his baldness, Bilko becomes anxious when Sergeant Joan Hogan throws him over for a wavy-haired corporal. He goes again to Tony his barber, who has been using Bilko's scalp as a testing ground for various restorers for seven years. One seems to work with spectacular results – until Bilko has a shampoo.

The Con Men 1 May 1956 3530

Written by Nat Hiken and Tony Webster

Three card sharps manage to swindle Private Doberman out of a $500 windfall as he is on his way to the bank. Bilko vows revenge, plays dumb when he finds the con men but then takes them for more than Doberman lost. But Doberman is not so easily educated in prudence and within a minute of getting the money back hands it over to a stranger in exchange for the Roseville Hotel.

War Games 8 May 1956 3511

Written by Nat Hiken and Arnold Auerbach

Bilko is asked to be best man at the wedding of a National Guard commander's son. Unfortunately a mock battle is arranged between the army and the National Guard for the same night. Bilko avoids the war games by escaping through a barracks window, but is followed by his 'troops' who think he is leading them to the enemy.

Bilko in Wall Street   (A.k.a. 'Butterworth, Butterworth & Butterworth')15 May 1956 3534

Written by Nat Hiken and Tony Webster

Bilko thinks his old army buddy, Morgan Twinhazy, is a big man on Wall Street and arrives in New York expecting to be whisked off on a Bermuda cruise. When Twinhazy turns out to be a $42-a-week drudge for a bank, Bilko helps him get on – fast. He poses as a spy from another bank, gets Twinhazy fired and rehired at $300 a week. Bilko also gets himself invited on a Bermuda cruise by the bank's senior partner.

Second Series

Produced and staged by Nat Hiken

Directed by Al de Caprio
Photographed by William J. Miller
Supervised by Edward J. Montagne
Editor: Ray Sandiford
Art Director: Richard Jackson
(Additional Art Direction by Robert Rowe Paddock)
Production Manager: M. Clay Adams
Music: John Strauss
Additional Music: Hank Sylvern
Recording Engineer: James Shields
Assistant to Producer: Kevin Pynes
Settings: Jack Landau
Additional Staging: Charles Friedman
Filmed by Kenco Films Inc.

Platoon in the Movies   18 September 1956 3535

Written by Nat Hiken, Tony Webster and Billy Friedberg

Bilko's motor pool are chosen to make an army training film on spark plugs, with Private Doberman playing the incompetent klutz, Private All-Thumbs. Doberman keeps fainting with stage fright every time the cameras roll. During a break, Bilko takes the opportunity to produce his own training film, 'What Every Young Spark Plug Should Know', with WAC dancing girls. The education officers are furious, but the Pentagon loves it.

It's for the Birds (A.k.a. 'The $64,000 Question') 25 September 1956 3536

Written by Nat Hiken and Billy Friedberg

Impressed by the money available on TV game shows, Bilko searches for an army candidate for 'The $64,000 Question'. He finds Private Honnegar once memorized a book on birds while snowbound on an Arctic expedition and fast-talks him into appearing on the show. He is performing brilliantly and has won $32,000 when an accidental blow on the head causes him to forget all he knows about birds. To save the army's reputation (and win the jackpot) Bilko rigs up a walkie-talkie link between the isolation booth and the textbook-primed platoon.

Bilko Goes to College   2 October 1956 3537

Written by Nat Hiken, Leonard Stern, Tony Webster and

Billy Friedberg

Bilko and his motor pool are sent to small Schmill College to teach the ROTC students vehicle maintenance. In order to teach a local gangster a lesson Bilko makes a 1000–1 bet with him that Schmill's football team will beat NotreDame, the champions, in the seasons's opener. Although he knows he hasn't a chance, Bilko organizes a publicity campaign for the team that has the gangster so nervous that he offers $10,000 to cancel the bet.

The Girl from Italy   9 October 1956 3541
Written by Nat Hiken

In New York, Bilko helps Rocco out with a family crisis: Rocco's brother, Angie, engaged to an Italian peasant girl when young refuses to marry her now she's come to the United States. Bilko's strategy is to glamourize her, *à la* 'My Fair Lady', to make Angie jealous. It works so well that Bilko falls for her himself.

The Face on the Recruiting Poster   16 October 1956 3540
Written by Nat Hiken, Tony Webster, Leonard Stern and Billy Friedberg

Handsome new recruit Mike McClusty's mysterious power over women encourages Bilko to turn him into a movie star. He starts by trying to get McClusty's face on an army recruiting poster. Doberman helps McClusty cram for the qualifying examination, and when Doberman passes instead of McClusty no one has the heart to tell him that his face is not exactly suitable for a recruiting poster. When Bilko and Doberman arrive in Washington, however, they find that the general who is to take the final decision looks remarkably like Doberman.

Bilko's War Against Culture   23 October 1956 3538
Written by Aaron Rubin, Phil Sharp and Nat Hiken

Bilko becomes desperate when his men give up gambling to attend art and dance classes run by Special Services – two beautiful women, a blonde lieutenant and her red-headed assistant. He fights back by arranging his money-making operations in the cultural events, but so cleverly that neither the Special Services officer nor Colonel Hall get wise.

A Mess Sergeant Can't Win   13 November 1956 3543

Written by Nat Hiken, Tony Webster, Billy Friedberg and Leonard Stern

Mess Sergeant Ritzik, about to leave the army, won't say goodbye to Bilko for fear of losing his $400 nest egg to him. Hurt by these suspicions, Bilko auctions off his personal belongings to raise $400 as a gift, but Ritzik is afraid to accept it. Bilko then bets Ritzik that Colonel and Mrs Hall are separating on their twenty-fifth wedding anniversary, but a domestic rift wins the bet for Bilko. He then bets Ritzik that his name isn't Ritzik, and the sergeant is so overjoyed at winning a bet with Bilko that he signs up in the army again.

Doberman's Sister   20 November 1956 3544

Written by Nat Hiken, Tony Webster, Leonard Stern and Billy Friedberg

It's family day at Fort Baxter and Bilko starts arranging dates for his platoon with some of the men's sisters. No one, however, wants to go out with Doberman's sister, Diane. Bilko persuades Zimmerman that she is a raving beauty so successfully that he ends up believing it himself. He fixes Zimmerman up with his own date, Sergeant Joan Hogan, and then discovers that Diane is Doberman's *twin* sister.

Where There's a Will   27 November 1956 3545

Written by Nat Hiken, Leonard Stern, Tony Webster and Billy Friedberg

An old buddy of Bilko's, Greg Chickering, is cut off by his late uncle with a single dollar and a one-eyed parrot called Cyclops and asks for his former sergeant's help. Taking three of his men with him, Bilko visits the stingy cousins and pretends that he is a treasure-seeker. He convinces them that the parrot holds the clue to a treasure map and they rush off to buy the bird from Chickering. On his return, however, Bilko finds his story was too convincing, that Chickering believed it and refused to sell Cyclops.

Bilko's Tax Trouble   4 December 1956 3546

Written by Nat Hiken, Leonard Stern, Tony Webster and Billy Friedberg

Bilko is accidentally called to explain his earnings to the income tax investigators through an administrative error. Bilko thinks he is under attack for his rackets and protest so much that the tax department decide to search further into Bilko's 'charities' for his men and he has to prove that he made no profit from them.

Mink Incorporated   11 December 1956 3547

Bilko loses $100 of the platoon's treasury on a horse race and decides to pay it back on the proceeds from a mink farm. He borrows another $300 and, after obtaining a pair of breeding minks, sets up operations in Fort Baxter, breaking thirty-two regulations in the process. But no matter what he does, the minks refuse even to nod to each other.

Sergeant Bilko Presents Ed Sullivan   18 December 1956 3548

Talent scouts working on a 'Salute to the Army' sketch for 'The Ed Sullivan Show' find no talent at Fort Baxter. Ed Sullivan, however, insists on a Mid-West GI taking part and so when a jeep driver is needed for the finale, Bilko is offered the part. The sergeant thinks that he has been engaged to star in a big production number and, on arriving in New York, breaks into a rehearsal and orders work on a Spanish routine entitled 'Granada'.

Bilko Gets Some Sleep   25 December 1956 3549
Written by Nat Hiken, Tony Webster and Billy Friedberg

Unable to sleep because of his bad conscience, Bilko takes the advice of the camp psychiatrist, Captain Adams: he reforms, gives up gambling, gets up with the men, does his work. He manages to sleep soundly but the rest of the camp goes crazy with worry over what he might be planning and Captain Adams finds himself overwhelmed with patients.

The Blue Blood of the Bilkos   8 January 1957 3551
Written by Nat Hiken, Billy Friedberg and Tony Webster

The son of a Fort Baxter sergeant is to marry a Philadelphia Main Line heiress, but her snooty family refuse to invite the boy's father to the wedding because he is not a commissioned officer. Fighting mad, Bilko goes to Philadelphia, declaring that the sergeant will be begged to attend the wedding. Bilko's investigations turn up some embarrassing revelations about the blue-bloods.

The Song of the Motor Pool   30 October 1956 3542
Written by Nat Hiken, Billy Friedberg, Tony Webster and Leonard Stern

Undeterred when he is turned down for an army musical

because he has no new material, Bilko discovers Private Paparelli humming a self-composed tune in the shower. He decides to make it into the Motor Corps new official song. Paparelli can only sing it in the shower however, so Bilko records it there, puts the song on paper and has the platoon hum it around Colonel Hall until he comes to believe he wrote it. The colonel then re-enters Bilko's men in the talent contest, where they are preceded by a Signal Corps unit singing the selfsame tune.

Bilko's Engagement   6 November 1956 3539
Written by Nat Hiken, Leonard Stern, Billy Friedberg and Tony Webster

Through a mix-up of boxes at a jewellry shop, Bilko finds himself giving Sergeant Joan Hogan an engagement ring instead of a gold bracelet-charm. Before he can explain, she has told the whole camp who enthusiastically congratulate Bilko. He is further trapped when Joan's relatives arrive and Colonel Hall holds a reception for the couple. Desperate he casts around for some way of not having to walk up the aisle.

Love That Guardhouse   15 January 1957 3550
Written by Nat Hiken, Billy Friedberg, Arnie Rosen and Coleman Jacoby

Taunted by Bilko about his bad luck at gambling, Mess Sergeant Ritzik sneaks off to Las Vegas and turns $50 into $1500. When he returns Colonel Hall, in response to Emma Ritzik's pleas, locks him in the guardhouse to protect him from Bilko. Sergeants Bilko, Grover and Birch try so hard to break in that they start a 'Free Rupert Ritzik' riot which gets them thrown in the cooler. Bilko finally succeeds in getting the money away from Ritzik, but has a change of heart and ends up stopping Emma Ritzik from going to Las Vegas.

Sergeant Bilko Presents Bing Crosby   22 January 1957 3552
Written by Nat Hiken, Billy Friedberg, Arnie Rosen and Coleman Jacoby

In order to recoup a loss on the horses, Bilko tries to promote a Bing Crosby concert at Fort Baxter. When his machinations to lure Crosby there fall through he is obliged to find a lookalike and singalike to take his place. Bing Crosby (and his brother Everett) makes one of his rare television appearances on this show.

Bilko Goes to Monte Carlo   29 January 1957 3553
Written by Nat Hiken and Billy Friedberg

Bilko stays up five nights in a row and emerges from his room with a foolproof system for winning at roulette. The entire camp bankrolls him for a trip to Las Vegas, but Colonel Hall gets suspicious and declares Nevada off-limits. Bilko then sets off for Monte Carlo with air force help (and money) but finds on arrival that he can't bring himself to risk his friends' money.

Bilko Enters Politics   5 February 1957 3554
Written by Nat Hiken, Billy Friedberg, Coleman Jacoby and Arnie Rosen

When the mayor of Roseville won't play ball with Bilko over building a de luxe servicemen's centre, Bilko masterminds a brilliant campaign to elect Doberman as mayor. With slogans like 'I'm Insane About Duane' he steamrollers the opposition – at least he does until Doberman himself is allowed to address the voters.

Bilko's Television Idea   12 February 1957 3555
Written by Nat Hiken and Billy Friedberg

When the TV network decides that Buddy Bickford is losing his comic appeal they send him and two writers to Fort Baxter to research background for an army comedy. Bilko sees the opportunity to make a lot of money and tries to sell Bickford a series called 'Andrew Armstrong – Tree Surgeon', having primed the platoon to collapse with laughter at the mention of 'wood'.

The Son of Bilko   26 February 1957 3556
Written by Nat Hiken, Billy Friedberg, Arnie Rosen and Coleman Jacoby

Bilko's fatherly approach to the welfare of his men is put under severe strain when a young draftee, Private Perkins, is assigned to his platoon. Although Perkins has been thrown out of fourteen other camps, Bilko pities him until he starts a succession of practical jokes: blowing reveille in the early hours, forging Bilko's signature, pretending to be a girl in the showers. Bilko decides to turn the tables . . .

Rock'n'Roll Rookie (A.k.a. 'Rock'n'Roll Recruit') 5 March 1957 3557

Written by Nat Hiken and Billy Friedberg

When rock'n'roll star, Elvin Pelvin is drafted the army tries desperately to find somewhere for him safe from screaming fans. When he comes to Fort Baxter Bilko schemes to have him in his platoon and plans records and performances for the rookie – but finds it not so easy.

Bilko's Black Magic 19 March 1957 3558

Written by Nat Hiken, Tony Webster and Billy Friedberg

Bilko's platoon has a new member: Private Lester Mendelsohn who has been recently rescued from a Pacific island where he had been marooned since 1942. He receives $7 456.38 in back pay but to Bilko's chagrin loses it at poker not to him but Grover and Ritzik, the worst players on the post. Bilko swears revenge and spreads the rumour that Mendelsohn learnt voodoo on his island and the god Coombar curses those who take advantage of him.

Bilko Goes South 26 March 1957 3559

Written by Nat Hiken, Billy Friedberg and Lou Meltzer

The camp is suffering temperatures of − 20°, and Bilko and his platoon decide that sun-drenched Florida is the place to go. When they hear that an army singing contest's finals will be held in Fort Lauderdale, Florida, they arrange to have all contest forms sent to the motor pool. They sign the forms as they arrive, not realizing they are volunteering to be bitten by mosquitoes with a fatal disease. Even in the plush Florida hotels with constant room service they still don't suspect anything.

Bilko Goes Round the World 2 April 1957 3560

Written by Nat Hiken, Billy Friedberg and Tony Webster

Mike Todd gets a call from Bilko suggesting a promotion for his film *Around the World in Eighty Days*: a $20,000 prize for the first person to go round the world in eighty hours. Bilko intends to collect the prize himself with the aid of an air force friend, but at the airport inadvertently drops his Priority Emergency Baggage tag on a 10-year-old boy.

The Mess Hall Mess 9 April 1957 3560

Written by Nat Hiken, Billy Friedberg and Tony Webster

Tired of Mess Sergeant Ritzik's cooking, Bilko goes to a

French restaurant and discovers a casserole which he thinks will win the contest for the best new American dish. The French chef, Marcel, however closely guards his recipe and Bilko is obliged to try many methods – including planting spies, staging a hold-up, analysing food samples and grilling the chef's son at school. After obtaining the recipe he learns that the chef stole it from an American cook book.

The Secret Life of Sergeant Bilko   16 April 1957 3563
Written by Nat Hiken, Billy Friedberg and Terry Ryan

An investigative journalist from a New York paper makes a clandestine visit to Fort Baxter in search of a story that GIs are carelessly leaking defence secrets. Bilko and his platoon soon spot him and start to sell him such classified information as the plans of the camp's sewage disposal system, the list of men entered in the Fort Baxter snooker competition and diagrams of how Private Doberman's trousers are to be let out.

Radio Station B.I.L.K.O.   (A.k.a. 'Radio Station W B B H ') 23 April 1957 3563
Written by Nat Hiken, Billy Friedberg and Terry Ryan

When the local radio station in Roseville closes down, Bilko sees the chance to make some money using Signal Corps equipment. His men go on the air: Rupert Ritzik's 'Kitchen Magic Time', Duane Doberman's news analysis and Colonel Hall and his wife secretly recorded as a soap opera 'John's Original Wife'.

Bilko, the Marriage Broker   30 April 1957 3564
Written by Nat Hiken, Billy Friedman, Coleman Jacoby, Arnie Rosen and Terry Ryan

A new company commander, Lieutenant Wallace, is making the lives of Bilko and his men miserable with his eager beaver attitudes. They decide he will only be humanized by marriage and plan to marry him off to a new WAC officer, Lieutenant Rogers. Unfortunately their attempts to pair them off are made more difficult by the fact that the couple are already secretly engaged.

Bilko Acres   7 May 1957 3566
Written by Nat Hiken and Billy Friedberg

Throughout Fort Baxter a rumour spreads that the GIs are

to be shipped overseas and the camp abandoned. Bilko interprets this as a sign that Fort Baxter is to be enlarged, and accordingly buys twenty-five acres of adjacent swamp with the platoon's welfare fund in the hope of making a killing when expansion plans are announced. Colonel Hall then tells him that the Pentagon wants to cut the size of the camp by ten acres.

The Big Scandal   14 May 1957 3565

Written by Nat Hiken, Billy Friedberg and Tony Webster

Bilko sees a chance of money in hypnotism after watching a professional at work. He practises on Sergeant Ritzik and tries to make him fall passionately in love with Colonel Hall's wife, Nell. Ritzik laughs in Bilko's face, but Private Doberman has inadvertently succumbed and starts a series of anonymous calls to Mrs Hall, declaring his love. Bilko takes it upon himself to save the colonel's marriage.

Bilko's Perfect Day   21 May 1957 3567

Written by Nat Hiken, Billy Friedberg and Terry Ryan

It finally happens: the shower is hot only for Bilko, Bilko guesses correctly the number of jelly beans in the jar winning first prize for Doberman, his ligher works for the first time in six years, he picks at random eight winners in eight horse races. His lucky day has arrived and he starts a race to raise money to bet on a wrestling match in San Francisco and a horse race in Australia. He finally gets into a poker game – which is immediately raided.

The Colonel Breaks Par   28 May 1957 3569

Written by Sydney Zelinka, Andrew Russel, Nat Hiken and Billy Friedberg

Colonel Hall decides not to take his fortnight's vacation and thus deprives Bilko of trouble-free time for making money. He schemes, therefore, to get the colonel to enter the officers' golfing tournament in Palm Springs and enlists the aid of his old army buddy, Sam Snead. Bilko suggests to the colonel that he swing with his eyes shut – when he does Snead hits the ball for him. After shooting 18 holes 11 under par the colonel can't wait to get to Palm Springs.

Show Segments   (A.k.a. 'Show Elements') 4 June 1957 3570

Several of the cast of 'The Phil Silvers Show' meet in Lindy's restaurant in Broadway for a snack before rehearsal. They meet Ed Sullivan and together watch various scenes from previous shows cut because they were too long for the half-hour format.

His Highness, Doberman   11 June 1957 3671

Private Doberman starts dating Lillian Middleton, the buxom and not-too-attractive daughter of a Roseville millionaire, but is thrown out of her parents' house when her mother discovers he is only a soldier. Bilko is enraged at this insult and, posing as a baron (with monocle), he bursts into the parents' house and orders them to keep their daughter away from 'His Highness, Crown Prince Doberman', who has joined the army incognito to study American military methods. The Middletons withdraw their ban and Bilko organizes a big party for the lovers.

Third Series

Produced by Edward J. Montagne

Staged by Aaron Ruben
Directed by Al de Caprio
Writing supervised by Billy Friedberg
Photographed by William J. Miller
Supervised by Edward J. Montagne
Editor: Ray Sandiford
Art Director: Richard Jackson
(Additional Art Direction by Robert Rowe Paddock)
Production Manager: M. Clay Adams
Music: John Strauss
Additional Music: Hank Sylvern
Recording Engineer: James Shields
Assistant to Producer: Kevin Pynes
Settings: Jack Landau
Additional Staging: Charles Friedman
Filmed by Kenco Films Inc.

Bilko's Merry Widow   17 September 1957
Written by Nat Hiken and Billy Friedberg

After borrowing from the platoon welfare fund to bet on a horse, Bilko organizes his men and presents a satire on the Lehár operetta *The Merry Widow*. (This was the last writing credit of Nat Hiken, the show's original deviser and writer.)

Bilko's Boy's Town   24 September 1957 3573
Written by Phil Sharp and Terry Ryan

Bilko hopes to spend some time at the gambling tables of Las Vegas, but Colonel Hall orders him and his men to remain in camp and away from desert manoeuvres in Nevada. In order to make some money Bilko establishes a boys' camp at Fort Baxter – but finds a smart youth called Roger is as sharp as the sergeant in getting his own way.

Hillbilly Whiz   1 October 1957 3579
Written by Coleman Jacoby and Arnie Rosen

To Bilko's delight one of the new recruits in his platoon, a country boy called Hank Lumpkin, has an unerring aim in pitching rocks at targets. And he can do it with either arm. Bilko cooks up a scheme to sell him to the New York Yankees for $125,000 – many of the current baseball stars appear in the show. (Dick Van Dyke appears as Hank Lumpkin.)

Bilko's Valentine   4 October 1957 3575

Written by Phil Sharp and Terry Ryan

Bilko's girlfriend, Sergeant Joan Hogan, decides that Bilko's forgetting her on Valentine's Day is the last straw. She quits the army and goes home to Sumter, South Carolina. Bilko is distraught and persuades the colonel to let him organize a recruiting drive in Sumter. When he arrives he pitches the entire campaign at Joan – to the point where she even dreams of him in various unlikely guises.

The Big Man Hunt   15 October 1957 3572

Written by Phil Sharp and Terry Ryan

On his way to Toledo for the 'Poker Olympics', Bilko notices a picture in the newspaper. It is of Red Thompson, a GI whose life he saved on Saipan in World War Two. Thompson has now discovered an African diamond mine and is looking to reward the soldier who saved him. For fear of being taken in by phonies, he has withheld the soldier's name. Bilko hurries off the bus to visit Thompson.

Bilko's Double Life   22 October 1957 3576

Written by A. J. Russell and Sydney Zelinka

On furlough in New York with Rocco and Henshaw, Bilko is mistaken for his double, multi-millionaire Herbert Penfield III. He finds himself leading a luxurious life on Penfield's credit. Meanwhile Penfield himself is visiting relatives near Fort Baxter and discovers that being mistaken for Bilko is no joke.

Sergeant Bilko Presents   29 October 1957 3580

A new young recruit, Hugo Lockman, turns out to have a great talent for playwriting. Bilko sees himself as the producer of Broadway successes with the concessions taped but is unable to find the necessary finance. In desperation he persuades the army that it needs to run a playwriting contest in the belief that Lockman will win it hands down. The Pentagon however is deluged with scripts from army camps all over the country.

Bilko Talks in His Sleep   19 November 1957 3582

Written by Billy Friedberg, Terry Ryan and Phil Sharp

The devastating Bilko charm overpowers a Roseville waitress, Gladys, who is also the object of the affections of

Sergeants Ritzik and Grover. In an unguarded moment Bilko promises to take Gladys to the Cotillion Club for dinner – and in order to raise the money plans a 'guess the number of beans in the jar' contest which he has fixed. At this point, however, he starts talking in his sleep and his rival sergeants overhear him.

Cherokee Ernie   26 November 1957 3581

Written by Arnie Rosen, Coleman Jacoby, Phil Sharp and Terry Ryan

Bilko goes down to Tulsa with his buddy, Corporal Charlie Whiteagle, on leave to play poker and win some 'oil money'. While he is there, Charlie's parents are hauled up before the Bureau of Indian Affairs for some minor infraction. Bilko rushes to their defence – and has to be sworn in in order to be heard. As 'Bald Eagle' Bilko discovers a flaw in the Owitashi treaty that gives Tulsa back to the Indians.

Bilko Buys a Club   3 December 1957 3578

Written by Terry Sharp and Phil Ryan

As ever set on easy money Bilko plans a night club near Fort Baxter and decides on Twin Oak Flats, a stretch of derelict property. Having difficulty making the down payment, Bilko decides to approach an investment banker who is a National Guardsman and in the camp on manoeuvres. Unfortunately he is misinformed as to the identity of the banker and makes his play to a supermarket butcher.

Lieutenant Bilko   10 December 1957 3584

Written by Sydney Zelinka and A. J. Russell

Bilko is about to leave the army when a notification comes from the Pentagon asking him to sign a release from a battlefield commission which he was given for three hours in the Marianas in World War Two. He realizes that he is owed $14,000 back pay and decides to stay on. At this point a general arrives who is so impressed with Bilko's officer-like qualities that he chooses him for a mission to outer space.

Bilko at Bay   17 December 1957 3586

Written by A. J. Russell, Terry Ryan and Sydney Zelinka

Unable to borrow money for a furlough in New York, Bilko arranges 'meal ticket' visits across the country at the homes of platoon members on his way to the big city. However, at Doberman's mother's in Altoona, Philadelphia they become involved with some bank robbers who promptly use them as hostages in their attempt to escape from the police.

Bilko F.O.B. Detroit   24 December 1957 3574
Written by Sydney Zelinka and A. J. Russell

Bilko is spending some time with his platoon in Detroit, motor capital of the US, in order to pick up a consignment of trucks for the army. So that he can have more time to enjoy himself he makes all kinds of complaints to the auto-firm and even tries to sell a 'Do-it-yourself' kit to motor manufacturer Roger Bellman, which has already been turned down by the army six times. Lionized by beautiful women at Bellman's mansion, Bilko completely forgets why he is meant to be in Detroit.

Bilko and the Flying Saucers   31 December 1957 3583
Written by Coleman Jacoby and Arnie Rosen

Bilko has made a date with a beautiful young singer, Bonnie Morgan, at the Dee Cee Club in Washington, and conceives the idea of reporting flying saucers in order to be called to the Pentagon. However, when he tells Colonel Hall his story, the colonel is so convinced that he starts seeing UFOs and hearing little men from Mars.

Bilko and the Colonel's Secretary   1 January 1958 3588
Written by Phil Sharp, Terry Ryan, A. J. Russell and Sydney Zelinka

When the colonel's secretary is suddenly transferred to administration school, Bilko decides he will handpick her replacement – some friendly WAC who will keep Bilko's name and those of his platoon off the duty rosters. But his choice resents leaving her boyfriend and takes it out on Bilko and his platoon, putting them on every dirty detail. As a way out, Bilko enters her in the Miss Roseville contest: first prize – a free trip to Switzerland.

Doberman the Crooner   c. 10 January 1958 3590
Written by ?

A home-made record amazes the platoon when the crooning voice turns out to be Doberman's. Bilko, quick to spot a fast buck, appoints himself his manager and arranges some commercial recordings. It is then he discovers that Doberman can only sing when he has a cold, and in desperation Bilko signs him up for an army cold vaccine experiment. There are unforeseen results . . .

Bilko Presents Kay Kendall   17 January 1958
Written by Neil Simon and Terry Ryan
With Kay Kendall as herself.

Bilko's Cousin   24 January 1958 3585
Written by Terry Sharp and Phil Ryan

The imminent arrival at Fort Baxter of a cousin of Bilko's
fills Colonel Hall with foreboding and Bilko with a garru-
lous pride in the family qualities. When cousin Swifty
arrives, however, he proves to be very gullible – so much so
that Bilko finds Doberman trying to sell him an army rifle.
Bilko then decides to get Swifty out of camp fast. (Dick Van
Dyke appears as Swifty Bilko.)

Bilko's Pigeons   31 January 1958 3587
Written by Phil Sharp and Terry Ryan

A Pentagon order discontinues Fort Baxter's back-up
communication system – a flock of carrier pigeons – and
with it Bilko's source of income from racing them. He then
decides to sell them to wealthy George Collingsworth III
knowing full well that they will return to his roost at the
first opportunity. He tries to do the same to Sergeants Ritzik
and Grover and nearly gets away with it.

Cyrano de Bilko   11 February 1958 3591
Written by Terry Sharp and Phil Ryan

Bilko helps one of his recruits, Harold, to land a date with
Natalie, the girl of his dreams. When Bilko thinks she is a
schemer, he tries to extricate Harold and, in order to prove
her two-timing, woos her himself. What Bilko doesn't realize is that there are two Natalies – one a beautiful young
girl, the other her middle-aged aunt – and he finds himself
engaged to a woman who is deadly serious.

The Colonel's Reunion   17 February 1958 3592
Written by Coleman Jacoby and Arnie Rosen

Colonel Hall launches all-out war against Bilko's gambling
empire at Fort Baxter, and with 'Operation Moonbeam'
succeeds in a few days in flushing out gambling from the
barracks, the gunshed, the furnace room and even the motor
pool grease pit. Bilko fights back by getting the colonel out
of the way – he sends a telegram which gets the colonel

invited to a class reunion in Chicago.

Bilko Saves Ritzik's Marriage   22 February 1958 3593
Written by Arnie Rosen and Coleman Jacoby

Sergeant Ritzik is on his way home to Emma, his wife, to celebrate their fifteenth wedding anniversary when he makes the mistake of getting caught up in a poker session with Bilko. When he returns at dawn his understandably angry wife walks out on him. Bilko feels responsible and starts a campaign to save the marriage, which includes planting a blonde in Ritzik's house to make Emma jealous

Bilko, the Art Lover   5 March 1958 3594
Written by Terry Sharp and Phil Ryan

On furlough in New York, Bilko is staying at the luxurious mansion of old GI friend Carlisle Thompson, whose father is a wealthy shipper. Carlisle wants to be an artist, while his father wants him in the family business; they argue and Carlisle leaves the plush house to move to a cold water loft in Greenwich Village, taking Bilko with him. This change in circumstances encourages Bilko to bring about a reconciliation between father and son.

Bilko, the Genius   14 March 1958 3595
Written by Arnie Rosen and Coleman Jacoby

A stroke of luck takes Bilko to a special army camp where they train geniuses. He introduces them to gambling and they in turn bring their talents to the subject. A mathematician invents a foolproof method of picking every winner at Santa Anita racecourse, an electronic wizard builds a radio-transmitter so Bilko can talk with his men at Fort Baxter, and an engineer builds a rocket to carry bets to Rocco and Henshaw. The scheme backfires when Rocco and Henshaw are arrested on charges of suspected spying.

Bilko, Male Model   c. 19 March 1958 3596
Written by Arnie Rosen and Coleman Jacoby

In Chicago on a military mission, Bilko takes time out to go on the town and is photographed with a pretty girl. The picture appears in a national magazine and receives 10,000 letters asking about him. On the strength of this, an advertising agency believes Bilko has the face that the average man wants to identify with and sets out to test his commercial value in a survey.

The Colonel's Inheritance   4 April 1958 3597
Written by Phil Sharp, Terry Ryan and Paul Jordan

A relative's will leaves $5000 to Colonel Hall and Bilko by-passes the Military Police and arranges for the money to be banked by Rocco and Henshaw. While at the bank they overhear a supposedly sure-fire tip about plutonium stock and Bilko invests the $5000. The stock immediately collapses, leaving Bilko to make up the money before the colonel discovers the truth.

Bilko's Honeymoon   c. 9 April 1958 3598

Private Paparelli wins first prize in a contest: an all-expenses paid vacation in a smart Miami hotel. Bilko muscles in, only to discover that the contest was for newlyweds. Undeterred, he dresses Paparelli in a wig and a dress and they set off on their honeymoon. When Colonel Hall turns up in Miami, Bilko has to produce a real female bride – which he does, a boozy barmaid called Clara.

Bilko's Chinese Restaurant   25 April 1958 3599
Written by Arnie Rosen and Coleman Jacoby

Inspired by the example of a new recruit's father, who started on a shoestring and now runs a chain of Chinese restaurants, Bilko thinks, with Wong Lee's help, he can do the same. Bilko is teaching Mess Sergeant Ritzik the art of Chinese cuisine, when Pentagon representatives arrive looking for some soldiers for a PR job with the Chinese people of Macoochi island. They're sure they've found their man and send Bilko and crew off to miserable Macoochi.

Operation Love   30 April 1958 35101
Written by Arnie Rosen, Coleman Jacoby and Terry Ryan

Fort Baxter's WACs, angry with their boyfriends for spending so much time gambling with Bilko, get themselves transferred to other camps. Bilko, under pressure from his irate men, starts a recruitment campaign and even joins a women's poetry circle in the hope of finding potential members of the Women's Army Corps.

Bilko's TV Pilot   (A.k.a. 'Doberman, Cowboy Hero') 6 May 1958 35100
Written by Arnie Rosen and Coleman Jacoby

Montana Morgan, a young cowboy, joins the platoon and

Bilko gets the idea of building a Western pilot film for television around him. After sending some photos to the TV company however, he finds to his surprise that they are more interested in Doberman for a series. Bilko immediately switches his attention to 'Tex' Doberman and has the platoon make a pilot around him.

Bilko Retires From Gambling   13 May 1958 35102
Written by Arnie Rosen and Coleman Jacoby

Colonel Hall, in another of his periodic attempts to clean up Fort Baxter, hires a card expert to pose as a recruit. In a fixed game with Grover, Ritzik and Coogan and with a deck stacked by the expert, Bilko finds himself losing all his money to Ritzik, the worst poker player on the camp. Bilko begins to doubt his card-playing abilities.

Bilko's Vacation   23 May 1958 35103
Written by Terry Ryan and Neil Simon

In order to get himself a free vacation at Dimmeldorf Lodge, Bilko convinces his platoon that they should all go there. He even convinces Colonel Hall to vacation there. When they all realize that they have been hoodwinked by Bilko they decide to turn the tables on him.

Bilko's Insurance Company   30 May 1958 35104
Written by Arnie Rosen and Coleman Jacoby

A near motor accident at Fort Baxter gives Bilko the idea of starting an insurance business for all the men on the camp. The scheme works well and Bilko rakes in money hand over fist until he is tempted to extend his operations. He offers a special maternity benefits policy to a pretty WAC, Sally Fisher, who marries and leaves Bilko staring ruin in the face.

Bilko's Prize Poodle   3 June 1958 35105
Written by Neil Simon and Terry Ryan

A little poodle shows great affection for Private Doberman and Bilko sees the chance of winning $10,000 in a national dog show. The entire camp cooperates in grooming Louise for the show, which she wins, only to be disqualified when the judges discover an error in her registry papers and classify her a mongrel.

Bilko's School Days   c. 10 June 1958 35106
Written by Neil Simon and Terry Ryan

Bilko is about to apply for a transfer to a posting in the Pacific when he learns that Fort Baxter is to be the site of a new training school. Bilko decides to stay on in anticipation of welcoming 1500 new recruits with their cash to his poker school. This happy vision is shattered when it becomes clear that the school is not for ordinary GIs but for Military Policemen.

Joan's Big Romance   c. 24 June 1958 35107

Sergeant Joan Hogan decides that she's fed up playing second fiddle to Bilko's poker games and takes a furlough in Chicago. On the train there, she meets a wealthy playboy, Randy Vandermeer, who is dodging reporters and photographers. A picture of them together appears in a national magazine and stirs Bilko into action – he devises a plan to convince Joan he has grown despondent over her actions. (This was the last appearance of Elisabeth Fraser as Joan Hogan.)

Papa Bilko   18 July 1958 3577

Written by Billy Friedberg, Sydney Zelinka and A. J. Russell

When he was in France in World War Two, Bilko became the benefactor of a poor French family. They all called him 'Papa' including the little daughter. Now the daughter, Mignon, has grown into a young lady and has come to the United States and visits her 'Papa'. Bilko finds it difficult to explain away the nickname and also to protect Mignon from his platoon of wolves.

Fourth Series

Produced by Edward J. Montagne

Staged by Aaron Ruben
Directed by Al de Caprio
Photographed by William J. Miller
Supervised by Edward J. Montagne
Editor: Ray Sandiford
Art Director: Richard Jackson
(Additional Art Direction by Robert Rowe Paddock)
Production Manager: M. Clay Adams
Music: John Strauss
Additional Music: Hank Sylvern
Recording Engineer: James Shields
Assistant to Producer: Kevin Pynes
Settings: Jack Landau
Additional Staging: Charles Friedman
Filmed by Kenco Films Inc.

Gold Fever   23 September 1958 35108

Bilko thinks he has found a map showing the site of a secret gold mine and investigates the site near Grove City, California. He finds a highway is about to be built through an abandoned army camp, Camp Fremont, which lies over the site. In a succession of outrageous ploys, Bilko gets the camp reopened and Colonel Hall to volunteer as the post's new commander. Fort Baxter moves to Camp Fremont and Bilko starts digging only to find a different gold mine to the one he expected.

Bilko's Vampire   1 October 1958 35112

When Ritzik starts opting out of poker games to watch horror films, Bilko tries to scare him off them by convincing him he is turning into a vampire. The plan works so well that even the colonel thinks Ritzik is inhuman, and Bilko sees the chance to sell 'Count Ritzik of Transylvania' for big bucks to Hollywood.

Bilko's De Luxe Tours   8 October 1958 35109

The poor train service from Grove City to San Francisco inspires Bilko to go into the transportation business. He starts by joining the local Parent–Teacher Association and persuading them to sell their school bus to one of his men for $25. Competition hots up when the railway expands its schedule to five trains a day and Bilko offers his service to civilians.

103

Bilko the Potato Sack King   15 October 1958 35113
Written by Neil Simon and Terry Ryan

Unable to resist the $20,000 salary, Bilko leaves the army to become a sales manager for potato sacks. Another firm producing plastic bags soon puts Bilko's boss out of business, but before he returns to the security of the army Bilko does his best to get rid of his employer's stocks. He starts by trying to convince the army to make all its uniforms out of potato sacking.

Bilko Vs. Covington   22 October 1958 35110

Battle is engaged on a titanic scale when Bilko meets an equally astute operator, Sergeant J. J. Covington. In order to get Covington to put in for a transfer, Bilko starts a rumour about a cultured pearl discovery in Japan. Covington retaliates with a story of a new use for volcanic ash and Bilko falls for it, buying 30,000 tons of it through a friend in Japan. As the war escalates, nerves become frayed and the two men sign a truce – only to miss out on a big opportunity.

Bilko Joins the Navy   28 October 1958 35115
Written by Neil Simon and Terry Ryan

Bilko, Paparelli and Zimmerman are on a three-day pass in San Diego when they hear of a huge crap game. Disguised as sailors, they break into the game but are raided by the Shore Patrol and end up as cooks on an aircraft carrier off to Alaskan waters for six months. Bilko hits on the idea of getting home by convincing a lieutenant that the captain is mentally disturbed.

Bilko's Big Woman Hunt   5 November 1958 35111

It's love at first sight for Sergeant Bilko. When trapped in a hotel's broken lift he is comforted by a pretty dancing teacher and is immediately smitten. But before he recovers she disappears and Bilko goes to the police for help in finding her. Claiming she picked his pocket, he gets the police artist to draw her picture and then uses it to search for her. Mistaken for one of her suitors whom she is trying to avoid he keeps getting thrown out of her hotel.

The Bilkos and the Crosbys   12 November 1958
Written by Neil Simon and Terry Ryan

Bilko fantasizes what his life would be like if he, and not Bing, were father of the Crosby sons. (The episode features

Gary, Philip, Dennis and Lindsay Crosby as themselves.)

Bilko's Allergy 19 November 1958 35114

Bilko develops a mysterious allergy to playing cards which prevents him playing any poker – even sitting outside a window and relaying his bids by walkie-talkie. A doctor diagnoses the trouble as psychological, stemming from guilt over Bilko's treatment of Colonel Hall. In order to cure himself, Bilko arranges a testimonial dinner for the colonel, but the secret preparations lead the colonel to believe Bilko is trying to oust him from his post.

Bilko and the Chaplain 26 November 1958 35118

Written by Arnie Rosen and Coleman Jacoby

Bilko is in San Francisco and his date is accidentally spoiled by the chaplain who has been asked by Colonel Hall to keep an eye on him. The chaplain promises to explain things to the girl if Bilko will help him stop a real estate agent from closing down a boys' home. Bilko succeeds by impersonating a four-star general but is later picked up by the Military Police and thrown in jail – as is the chaplain.

Bilko Presents the McGuire Sisters 3 December 1958

Written by Phil Sharp and Terry Ryan

With Mickey Rooney and the McGuire Sisters as themselves.

Bilko's Secret Mission 10 December 1958 35120

Selected for a secret mission to Yucca Flats, Nevada, Bilko shrewdly appreciates that it is only forty miles from Las Vegas. He breaks out of the army compound with Sergeant Ritzik, possessor of an astrological method of winning at roulette. The pair win thousands of dollars but are arrested by the MPs before they can cash their winnings.

Bilko's Giveaway 17 December 1958 35116

In Hollywood with no money, Bilko teams up with a child genius on a quiz show and wins a great deal of merchandise but no cash. He can't pay the $6000 taxes due on the prizes, nor can he sell them profitably, so he starts an all-GI quiz show on the local TV station. Bilko feeds Doberman the answers and he becomes the resident genius and a local hero after week after week of success answering questions on his special subject: comic books.

Bilko and the Medium   22 December 1958 35121

Seeking the money to start a pool hall, Bilko visits the Ritziks who have just won $500 in a raffle. Since they only take financial advice from Madame Zaboda, a medium, Bilko arranges his own seance. His 'medium' Madame Flossie, a local manicurist, is exposed by Madame Zaboda. When Bilko learns Madame Zaboda intends stealing the Ritziks' money herself he is doubly eager to get his revenge on her.

Bilko's Bopster   1 January 1959 35122

When jazz drummer Skinny Sanders is assigned to his platoon, Bilko dreams of leading an all-army jazz band round Europe. Unfortunately the distinct lack of army talent obliges him to go to San Francisco and fast-talk Skinny's civilian buddies into the army. The band is formed, but instead of the Pentago sending Bilko to Europe, they order him to form a second band to tour the Pacific.

Bilko's Hollywood Romance   9 January 1959 35123

A fiery-tempered film star's press agent decides that the best thing for her image would be a romance with an ordinary soldier. Bilko wangles the position as Monica Malamar's latest flame, but back in Hollywood reveals his true nature which forces Monica's bosses to try and get rid of him. They build him up as a star in his own right, planning to drop him later but find that he seems to be taking over the entire studio.

Bilko's Grand Hotel   28 January 1959 35124

Just as Bilko is about to open a pizza stand, Privates Paparelli and Zimmerman get careless and burn it down. Undaunted, Bilko buys a derelict hotel, puts a pan-handler called Chester Hilton in charge, renames it the Grove City Hilton and waits for Hilton Hotels to pay him to close it down. Just as he is about to be paid $5000 for the hotel Paparelli and Zimmerman get careless again . . .

Bilko's Credit Card   4 February 1959 35125

Bilko dreams up the GIs Gourmet Guild, a credit card for Camp Fremont GIs. He signs up all the local bars and restaurants and encourages members by spreading a rumour that Mess Sergeant Ritzik has a contagious disease. But when the first payment is due all the men are called out on surprise early-morning manoeuvres, leaving Bilko

$5000 in debt. He impersonates a visiting British officer and causes havoc at the military exercises, thus ending them and allowing him to collect his money.

Viva Bilko   11 February 1959 35126

Bilko and three privates, Paparelli, Zimmerman and Doberman, visit Mexico and are held up and robbed of their clothes. The robbers go on to hold up a bank dressed in the soldiers' uniforms. Recovering their clothes later, Bilko and his buddies are arrested as bank robbers. The confusion clears only long enough for them to get back across the border to be arrested by the MPs for overstaying their three-day passes.

The Colonel's Promotion   18 February 1959 35127

Written by Arnie Rosen and Coleman Jacoby

Hoping for a promotion, Colonel Hall starts a clean-up drive at Camp Fremont which forces Bilko to use radar in order to spot the colonel about to break up a poker game. When no promotion comes, Bilko goads Colonel Hall into going straight to the Pentagon. Mrs Hall asks Bilko to go along too and keep him in check. In Washington, Bilko tries to include the colonel in President Eisenhower's golf foursome as the quickest way of promotion.

Bilko's Sharpshooter   25 February 1959 35128

Bilko discovers a sharpshooting WAC Polly Porter and starts promoting her as a new Annie Oakley. He launches her career by signing her up for a shooting contest against Sergeant Ritzik's marksman, Private Masters. When they meet on the rifle range, however, it's love at first sight and both their aims are spoiled.

Bilko's Formula Seven   4 March 1959 35129

The accidental mixture of applejack and crankcase oil on Private Jenkins' face seems to remove wrinkles, and Bilko is quick to spot the commercial possibilities. Naming it 'Bilko's Formula Seven' he markets it with a filmed commercial showing the effect on Sergeant Ritzik's wife, Emma. He is on the point of selling the formula to cosmetics manufacturer, Deborah Darling, when Jenkins and Emma Ritzik burst in with the news that the effects are only temporary. Bilko gets excited again when his men fool him into believing that the mixture grows hair.

Bilko's Ape Man   18 March 1959 35131

Bilko hopes to launch Private Forbes, a former physical training teacher, in a film career, and enters him in a 'Mr Universe' contest. Bilko is thrown out for trying to bribe a judge. He then tries to make a film of Forbes fighting a gorilla (Doberman in costume). The colonel catches sight of Doberman and sends out troops with flame-throwers. Bilko saves Doberman, but Forbes, waiting in the woods, mistakes the colonel for the gorilla.

Warrant Officer Paparelli   25 March 1959 35130

Fed up with a new lieutenant's rule-book discipline, Bilko hatches the idea of getting one of his own men promoted to officer in charge of the motor pool. He arranges that Paparelli 'saves' the life of a visiting general three times in one day and gets promoted on the spot. But Lieutenant Paparelli, inspired by the colonel, starts cracking down on Bilko and he needs a quick flash of inspiration to demote the monster he has created.

Bilko's Godson   3 April 1959 35132

Filled with pride at being named a godfather to the son of a GI friend, Bilko decides to do something for him: get him enrolled in Stanford University's class of 1977. He learns that only children of Stanford students or graduates can be enrolled so far in advance, so he sits the entrance exams. To make sure he passes he gets Fleischman to take history, Turk, the bookmaker, to take maths and Moose, a bootlegger, to do science. The proble is getting them into the examination hall . . .

Guinea Pig Bilko   17 April 1959 35133

Colonel Hall is filled with glee when he tricks Bilko into taking a new tranquillizer pill which the Pentagon wishes to test. It robs Bilko of his love for money; his men, however, take over his schemes and prove even more rapacious. The colonel decides he prefers one Bilko to a camp of them and decides to shock him out of his placidity by asking him to count all the money in the camp treasury.

Bilko the Butler   24 April 1959 35134

A friend of Bilko marries a rich socialite whom he met through the USO and the sergeant decides he will emulate the feat. At the San Francisco USO he turns down dinner on a fishing boat to dine at Nob Hill mansion. The hosts are the butler and his wife but Bilko wangles himself into a millionaire's cocktail party as a waiter. He overhears a stock market tip and calls Henshaw to get him to invest all his savings. Then he discovers it was a phoney tip and can't get hold of Henshaw . . .

Ritzik Goes Civilian 1 May 1959 35135

Emma Ritzik persuades her husband to leave the army and open a roadside diner, instead of losing all his money to Bilko at poker. Bilko's men shun him for causing Ritzik to leave, so he visits the couple and finds they were swindled over their diner. He helps them get their money back, but has to convince Emma Ritzik that he is leaving the army before she will let her husband sign up again.

Bilko's Small Car 8 May 1959 35136

The police in Grove City seize Colonel Hall's European sports car which Bilko had 'borrowed' to transport gambling equipment. To cover up, Bilko converts a jeep into a similar sports car; the result provokes so much comment that the sergeant goes into the motor business and immediately sells ten cars. This means, however, that they need to explain where ten jeeps went . . .

Doberman, Missing Heir 15 May 1959 35137
Written by Arnie Rosen and Coleman Jacoby

With Bilko's help a millionaire couple, Lord and Lady Rockford, discover their long-lost son and heir, Duane Doberman. They money turns Doberman's head and he refuses to help his army buddies. In order to get some money, Bilko plans to marry Doberman to Dixie Darcel, a striptease dancer, who will share the money with him after the wedding. But he has to find a way to get rid of her fast after the Rockfords find out that Doberman is not really their child.

Bilko's Casino 20 May 1959 35138

An old document which comes into Bilko's possession seems to exempt the site of the Grove City USO from California's anti-gambling laws. He buys the building and is about to open a casino when a big gambling syndicate starts to muscle in. Bilko tried to frighten them away by pretending that Doberman is an FBI agent hot on their trail, but things don't quite turn out as he's planned . . .

The Colonel's Second Honeymoon   29 May 1959 35139

Written by Arnie Rosen and Coleman Jacoby

Refused a furlough by Colonel Hall, Bilko contrives a fight between the colonel and his wife and then suggests they make it up and go on a second honeymoon. When they go, Bilko wangles his furlough papers from Captain Barker and sets off for Sun Valley. He finds himself at the same hotel as the Halls who are still angry with each other and he manages to bring about a reconciliation.

Bilko in Outer Space   5 June 1959 35140

Written by Neil Simon and Terry Ryan

Sergeants Ritzik and Grover have won $600 and are terrified of losing it to Bilko. They sleep in the woods at night, install an alarm system in the mess hall and spend a day hiding in the freezer. Bilko tries starting a poker game by telephone and in disguise but fails. Finally he builds a dummy space chamber and tricks the sergeants into volunteering for a three-day space indoctrination test.

The Bilko Boycott   12 June 1959 35141

Tired of losing his money to Bilko, Corporal Henshaw sets up Gamblers' Anonymous in Camp Fremont which drastically cuts Bilko's income. He starts looking around for new customers and succeeds with the WACs. Through a series of motor maintenance lectures, Bilko manage to removes their pay from the girls, but comes down with measles and is put in quarantine after invading their barracks to collect.

Weekend Colonel   17 June 1959 35142

Written by Neil Simon and Terry Ryan

A network of closed circuit television cameras allows the colonel to clean up gambling at Camp Fremont. When the colonel goes off for the weekend, Bilko installs a short order chef, Charlie Klusterman, the colonel's double as the camp commander and gets him to remove the TV equipment and to authorize a Monte Carlo night at the Officers' Club. Then the real Colonel Hall comes home unexpectedly . . .

Acknowledgements

The authors would like to thank Susan Hill, whose idea this was in the first place; Jim Cochrane, who nursed it through its infancy; Viacom, who provided all the script material; Nick Jones, at the BBC for his help and patience, and Jane and Clare for theirs.

Most of all, thanks to Phil Silvers, without whom . . .